Great Preachers on

The Prodigal Son

~ ※ ~

Dead, and Alive Again, Lost, and Found.

By

D. L. MOODY

C. H. SPURGEON

HENRY MOORHOUSE

W. HAY HITKEN

T. DEWITT TALMAGE

From the 1896 Edition

~ ※ ~

TABLE OF CONTENTS

THE PRODIGAL SON | THE PARABLE

A certain man had two sons.

And the younger of them said to his father, "Father, give me the portion of goods that falleth to me."

And he divided unto them his living.

And not many days after, the younger son gathered all together, and took his journey into a far country, and there wasted his substance with riotous living.

And when he had spent all, there arose a mighty famine in that land; and he began to be in want. And he went and joined himself to a citizen of that country; and he sent him into his fields to feed swine. And he would fain have filled his belly with the husks that the swine did eat: and no man gave unto him.

And when he came to himself, he said, "How many hired servants of my father's have bread enough and to spare, and I perish with hunger! I will arise and go to my father, and will say unto him, Father, I have sinned against heaven, and before thee, and am no more worthy to be called thy son: make me as one of thy hired servants."

And he arose, and came to his father.

But when he was yet a great way off, his father saw him, and had compassion, and ran, and fell on his neck, and kissed him.

And the son said unto him, "Father, I have sinned against heaven, and in thy sight, and am no more worthy to be called thy son."

But the father said to his servants, "Bring forth the best robe, and put it on him; and put a ring on his hand, and shoes on his feet. And bring hither the fatted calf, and kill it; and let us eat, and be merry: For this my son was dead, and is alive again; he was lost, and is found."

And they began to be merry.

CHOICE THOUGHTS FROM MANY MINDS

A certain man had two sons. And the younger of them said to his father: "Father, give me the portion of goods that falleth to me."

Such a request showed his discontented state of mind.

Desiring to be one's own master is the beginning of all sin.

And he divided unto them his living.

The father did not do anything to restrain or punish his son. He just left him to sow and then to reap.

The sequel shows that we may be thankful that all our prayers are not answered.

And not many days after, the younger son gathered all together,—

Here we see the prosperous prodigal, for remember—he was as much a prodigal the moment he turned his back on his father as when later he was feeding swine.

and took his journey—

A man reaches the depths of ungodliness by stages.

It is a "journey." Some travel more quickly than others, but all arrive at the same dark destination.

into a far country,—

. . . far from his father, from home restraints, from good influences.

His heart having already gone into the far country, he followed. The way is downwards, downhill.

Homelessness, farness from God, is man's state by nature. It is not measured in space, but in the affections.

and there wasted his substance—

He had a fortune in his hand, not in his head or heart. Any fool can squander the former, but not the latter.

with riotous living.

The story has often been repeated literally. Too often when men forsake God, they turn to sensual gratification, uncontrolled by thoughts of God and directed solely to earthly excitements.

Riotous living—the deadliest way to exhaust the body, debase the mind, destroy the substance, and damn the soul.

And when he had spent all,—

. . . without gaining any substantial returns.

Probably in a short time. Sinful pleasure is brief.

there arose a mighty famine in that land,—

Such men help to bring about famines,—those who are always consuming and wasting, and never producing.

This famine was the external cause of the prodigal's return. God allows human circumstances to hasten the consequences of sin. Famines and other miseries are messengers He sends after His wandering children.

The saddest famine of all is that of the soul.

and he began to be in want.

He had now begun to realize that the pleasures of sin are only for a season. He had got all the world could give him, and then found himself in want.

This is the main point. When the wandering sinner *feels* his *want*, he must either despair or repent.

And he went and joined himself to a citizen of that country;—

The young man who sought freedom from a father's control came into abject dependence upon a stranger.

and he sent him into his fields to feed swine.

He would not live with his father; now he was compelled to live with swine.

Shame, contempt and distress are wedded to sin, and can never be divorced.

He who will not be a son to the Heavenly Father must be a slave to the devil.

There is no master so cruel as Satan, no yoke so heavy as sin.

And he would fain have filled his belly—

And even then he would not have *satisfied* his belly—;

with the husks that the swine did eat.

The swine were better off than the prodigal, because husks did nourish them, and they got their fill.

He sold himself to the devil, and all he got was—husks!

Sensual pleasures *fill*, but *never satisfy*.

When we see men at fifty, or even sixty, years of age, still feverish about some new pleasure, we see a soul formed with a capacity for high and noble things, fit for the banquet-table of God Himself, trying to fill its infinite hollowness with husks.

And no man gave unto him.

With all his banquets and rioting, he had not gained one true friend.

And when he came to himself,—

A brighter day now began to dawn after the terrible night.

He began to realize (1) his present bad lot, (2) what it might be.

After all, there is in every man something better than a fool, a spendthrift, a hog-tender. A man's real self is never satisfied with sinning and sinking; he knows he is fitted for something better and purer.

he said, "How many hired servants of my father's have bread enough and to spare, and I perish with hunger."

Perhaps it was only his stomach, then, and not his conscience, that urged him homewards. But low as this motive would be, it was enough. So long as any motive brings you home to God through faith in Christ Jesus, it is a blessed one.

His will took him away; his wants brought him back.

"I will arise and go to my father, and will say unto him, Father, I have sinned against heaven and before thee,—

He acknowledged that he was without excuse. He had not a word to say about his "failures," his "faults," his "wild oats," etc. He called it by the right name—Sin.

He showed a proper appreciation of the nature of his sin—first, against God; then, against his father.

"And am no more worthy to be called thy son. Make me as one of thy hired servants."

He went out as a son. He would be glad to return as a servant.

It is the glory of the Gospel that it is the refuge, the last resource, of the broken hearted. God does not reject the jaded heart.

And he arose,—

. . . feeling how low down he was morally.

Resolve results in action.

This is where repentance merges, into faith.

and came to his father.

What did it mean? There was before him along and weary journey which he (who had been brought up in plenty) had to face without means. There was the humiliation of the confession of his sin, of the position as a servant. But true repentance was willing to face all this.

Departure from God is the essence of all sin; return to God is the essence of true repentance.

But when he was yet a great way off, his father saw him,—

. . . before he saw his father. Love is far-sighted. The eyes of mercy are quicker than the eyes of repentance. Even the eye of faith is dim compared with the eye of God's love. He sees the returning sinner before the sinner sees him.

and had compassion,—

No depths were too low for the father's love to reach.

and ran,—

So God is *in a hurry* to welcome the returning prodigal.

Slow are the steps of repentance, but swift are the feet of forgiveness.

and fell on his neck, and kissed him.

He did not delay a moment, for though he was out of breath, he was not out of love.

The Scotch call this "The Parable of the Wonderful Father." There are many such sons, but not always such a father.

And the son said unto him, "Father,—

. . . the most obvious sign of his repentance was recognizing his father as father.

"I have sinned against heaven, and in thy sight, and am no more worthy to be called thy son."

But the father said to his servants, "Bring forth the best robe, and put it on him, and put a ring on his hand, and shoes on his feet; and bring hither the fatted calf, and kill it; and let us eat and be merry; for this my son was dead and is alive again; he was lost, and is found."

Heaven keeps holiday when some poor waif comes shrinking back to the Father.

And they began to be merry.

And we are not told that they ever left off! The conversion of a soul is enough to make everlasting joy in the hearts of the righteous.

THE PRODIGAL SON | By D. L. MOODY

This young man, the prodigal son, started wrong—that was the trouble with him. He was like hundreds and thousands of young men in our cities today who have a false idea of life: and when a man has a false idea of life, it is very hard for his father or mother or any of his friends to do anything with him.

I do not know where his mother was. Perhaps he had sent her to the grave with a broken heart. The Lord did not speak of his mother; if she had been living, He would have probably referred to her.

The father is to be censured; we cannot help but blame the father. When the son said, "Father, divide, and give me my portion," the father should have said:

"You show a bad spirit. I will let you go without your portion."

A great many fathers make that mistake now. I do not think this father could have done a greater unkindness to the boy than to give him his goods and money, and let him go. It showed a contemptible spirit in the boy when he came to his father and said:

"Divide: give me my portion and let me go."

He wanted to go away from his father's prayers and influence, and get into a foreign land where he could go on as he pleased, where he could run riot and plunge into all kinds of sin, and where there was no restraint. And that indulgent father gratified his wish, and divided his goods with him. I have two sons, and if either should ask me for a portion I'd say:

"Go and earn it by the sweat of your brow."

Of all classes I most pity rich men's sons with nothing to do. It's a good deal better for your sons to earn wealth or themselves than for you to earn it for them. I have more respect for a rich man's son who makes anything of himself than for a poor man's son. Self-made men are the only men good for anything. The rich men's sons are spoilt. Their fathers do everything, even their thinking, for them. They are subject to all kinds of temptations, which poor men's sons never know.

Perhaps this young man did not get on well with his older brother. Or perhaps he grew restive under home restraints. We are not told the reason why he left home, but not many days after he had received his portion, he went around to his old companions and bade them all good-bye, and went off to a foreign country, perhaps to Egypt. He started out with a false idea of life; nine-tenths of the young men do. He thought he'd find better friends and have a better time in that far off country.

How Satan blinds men! With some it is money; with others pleasure; with all of us, it is selfishness under one form or another.

He started off, holding his head very high that morning. He was full of pride and conceit, and he had very lofty ideas. If anyone had told him what he was coming to, he would have laughed in scorn. But mind you once a man starts on the downward track, he will sink lower and lower, unless by the grace of God he turns from sin to righteousness. The first lie, the first drink, the first petty theft, is often

A CRISIS IN A MAN'S LIFE.

I suppose, like young men of today, he went to Memphis or some other large city. He put up at the best hotel, he smoked the best cigars, he drank none but the best wines and drove none but the fastest horses. He did not mix with the common men. He gathered a number of choice friends around him, and thought he was having a high time. The very first thing we hear of him is, he is in bad company. He began to waste his substance in riotous living. I never knew a young man who treated his father unkindly who would not go off into bad company. We hear of him going on in all kinds of vice. He devoured his living with harlots. He was guilty of adultery—the shortest, quickest, surest road to ruin. If they had theaters in those days, (and I do not doubt but they had), he would be in the theater every night in the week. We should find him in the billiard-hall and the drinking saloon. We should find him in the ways of those whose feet take hold on hell. He was a popular young man; he had plenty of money, and his money was popular. He was a grand companion for the young men in that far country; they liked his society.

If you had asked him to come to a religious meeting, he would have been indignant. What need had he of a Savior? What did he care for his father's Bible or his mother's prayers?

That first year he was very independent. He had a great many admirers fluttering around him. His friends were the leading young men—the upper ten. He moved in very high circles. The aristocratic mothers were foolish enough to introduce their daughters to him; they were very glad to make his acquaintance.

That was the first year, but he cleared it all out in five years or less. Perhaps his portion was $100,000. It does not take long for a young man to go to ruin when he gets among harlots and wild young fellows. It takes one generation to accumulate, the next spends it.

Where are his friends now? He had plenty to gamble with him at first. They liked to take a helping hand in spending his money; but gradually he hasn't money enough to pay the tailor. He is getting a little shabby in appearance. His clothes are not so good as they were. He once had a good wardrobe, but now he goes to the pawn-shop, and he pawns his overcoat for strong drink; and one thing after another soon goes. He might have had some gift which his mother gave him when she was dying, and at last that goes; and yet he does not come to himself. When he first came to Memphis he used to get drunk at least once a week. Now you see him hanging around the pawn-broker's. He asks one of his former friends to lend him a dollar. They were ready enough to strip him of his money; now they point him out as the biggest fool in all Memphis.

"He came here five years ago," one of them says, "with $100,000, and he's gone through the whole of it. He actually asked me to lend him a dollar. I wouldn't lend him a cent."

His friends were the friends of his circumstances. Give me the friend who is my friend for what I am, not for what I've got. I want a friend who will stand by me in the time of calamity.

He pawns his ring, the sign of sonship, and his clothes. And then a mighty famine strikes the land. There is always a famine in the devil's territory. A mighty famine struck the land, and this young man began to feel the want of food.

The fact is, it doesn't take long to drain the cup of pleasure dry. There may be pleasure in sin, but it does not last. It ends in want and misery every time. Satan never gives enduring satisfaction. When this young man got home they "began to be merry," but now in the far county he begins to be in want. And "no man gave unto him." Generosity is a virtue which does not flourish in that kind of soil.

ONE REDEEMING POINT.

He had one redeeming point—he would not beg or steal. God have mercy on a young man in perfect health who will beg! He is not far from being a thief.

The prodigal looked round for a job. Would any bank president have him for cashier? "I couldn't trust him," they would say. Would any leading merchant take him? "I couldn't," they would answer: "he has lost his character."

"Look at his hands," one said; "he can't earn anything at manual labor."

He went round for a number of days, and at last was hired to look after swine. He was so hungry that he would have eaten husks if he could have got them. No man gave him even husks. This wealthy man's son, who was brought up amid good influences and surroundings, is now living in that foreign country like a man who had never seen a decent home.

Now, just for a moment think what that man lost in all these years.

He lost his *home*; he had no home. His friends, when he had money, might have invited him around to their homes; but it was not home for him. There is not a prodigal upon the face of the earth but has lost his home. You may live in a gilded palace; but if God is not there, it is not home. If your conscience is lashing you, it is not home.

He lost his *food*. His father's table did not go to that country. He would have fed on the husks that the swine did eat. This world cannot satisfy the soul.

Then he lost his *testimony*. I can imagine that some of the young men of that country saw him among the swine, feeding them, and they said:

"Look at that poor wretched young man, with no shoes on his feet, and with such shabby garments."

They looked at him and called him a beggar, and pointed the finger of scorn at him.

He said: "You need not call me a beggar. My father is a wealthy man."

"Your father a wealthy man?"

"Yes."

"You look like a wealthy man's son!"

Not a man believed him when he said he was a wealthy man's son. His testimony was gone. So when a man goes into the service of the devil, he sinks lower and lower; and it is not long before every one loses confidence in him. One sin leads on to another. His testimony is gone.

He lost his *health*, his *good name*, his *time*.

And he did not gain much to compensate him for these losses. He got a good many things, however. He got the jeers of his former companions. He got rags and filth. He got a gnawing hunger, and a depraved appetite. He got a sad experience of the unsatisfying nature of worldly pleasures.

But there is

ONE THING HE DID NOT LOSE,

and if there is a poor backslider reading this, there is one thing you have not lost. That young man never lost *his father's love.*

I can imagine one of his father's neighbors met him in that place, and said to him:

"My boy, I have just come from your home. Your father wants you to return."

I can imagine the young man said: "Did my father speak of me? I thought he had forgotten me."

"Why," says the man, "he thinks of nothing else. He thinks of you day and night. Do you think he has forgotten you? No, never. He cannot forget you. He loves you too well for that."

One morning he got his work done sooner than usual, and got to thinking. I wish I could get men to think what they are and where they are going. His mind went back over his past conduct, and he saw nothing but sin. In the future he saw nothing but death and judgment. In his childhood days he remembers how he used to play with his brother, and how the old birch tree in front of the house looked. He remembers his mother used to bend over him at night and teach him some little prayer, such as, "Now I lay me down to sleep." He remembered the morning when he left home.

"Father tried to pray for me," he meditated, "but he couldn't finish his prayer. His grip was like a vice as he said, 'It's just breaking my heart to have you go. Remember, I shall always be glad to see you back. I hope you won't be away long.'

"If I stay here much longer, I'll starve to death, and they will bury me like a pauper. Here I am, perishing with hunger, while my father's hired servants have bread enough and to spare. I will arise and go to my father, and say to him, 'Father, I have sinned against heaven and before Thee.'"

ONE OF THE GREATEST BATTLES EVER FOUGHT

was being fought out then. Everything holy and heavenly was beckoning him home. The powers of darkness were trying to keep him from returning.

"You go back and they'll all laugh at you. What'll they say?" said the devil.

No doubt there was an angel hovering over him, watching for the decision, and when he arose and said, "I will arise," the angel bore it on high.

"Make another crown. Get another robe ready. There's another sinner coming!"

That "I will" echoed and re-echoed, and there was joy in the presence of the angels. He is saved already.

His heart has got home already. The battle with pride and sin is over.

As the Scripture puts it, "He came to himself." It is a grand thing to see a man coming to himself. When he began to come to himself, then it was there was hope for him. It teaches us clearly that all these years he had been out of his mind. Very likely he thought Christians were out of their minds. There is not a drunkard, harlot, thief, or gambler, but thinks Christians are mad; and they call us fanatics. But Solomon says: "Madness is in their heart while they live, and after that they go to the dead."

When he came to himself, he said: "I will perish here. I will arise and go to my father." That was the turning point in that young man's life. There is always hope for a man when he begins to think. I wish you would bear in mind that if you are willing to own your sin, and own that you have wandered from God, God is willing to receive you. The very moment you are willing to come, that moment God is willing and ready to receive you. He delights in forgiveness. I do not care how vile you have been, if you are willing to come back, God is willing and ready to receive you.

It did not take long, after his mind was made up, to go. He had no friends to visit and bid good-bye to. There was no one to love and pity him. He asked his employer to settle up—he didn't get much. He came just as he was—poor, ragged, dirty; he did not wait to get fixed up.

I see him as he starts for home. He has a hard journey. He is almost starved. Day after day he travels on. He has no fear of thieves, for he has squandered all he had.

If a man had seen him going along the road when he started for home, he'd have said: "There goes a tramp."

A tramp? He is an heir of glory, going to sit on the throne with Christ. He is already in the kingdom. If a man is not saved, it is not because he *can't*, but because he *won't*. The only obstacles in the way of receiving pardon for sins are those you make yourself.

One day he gets to the top of a hill—and then he's across the line. There is a strange feeling about getting back into your own country, under the old flag; there's an excitement about it. He gazed at a blue hill in the distance, and said to himself,

"When I get on that hill I can see how the old house looks."

When he arrives on that hill-top, how his eyes feast on the homestead!

Now let us take a look into the home. It is the hour of family worship. The old father reads a psalm, one of the psalms of David, the 91st or the 46th, perhaps. After reading, they sing, and the old man prays. He prays for the servants, the elder brother, the neighbors, then his voice begins to falter a little, and he prays:

"God bring home my wandering boy!"

That cry had gone up from that altar every evening for five years.

"Who's that your master was praying for?" you ask the servants.

"His youngest son."

"Why, I've lived here for three years, and never knew he had one. What kind of a young man is he?"

"A good-for-nothing, miserable wretch," they answer.

Then you enquire of the elder son.

"Yes, sir, I've a younger brother. He's off down at Memphis."

"Is he in business down there?"

"No, sir, my father gave him his fortune, and he spent it all with harlots and riotous living."

You notice it's the elder brother that says this. Not a bit will the father tell. Go and sit down by that gray-haired father and ask him,

"Would you forgive him?"

"Forgive him? Why, there's been nothing in my heart but love for him all along. Let him come home, and you'll see how gladly I'll restore him."

The father, in the parable, represents your God and mine. His heart is full of love for us, no matter how we turn our back on Him, and disobey. He so loved us that He sent His only begotten Son to die for us.

One day the old father is on the flat roof on the top of the house. It is about three o'clock in the afternoon. The old man is praying with his face turned towards Jerusalem. He takes his usual look along the highway, and sees a stranger in the distance. He holds up his hands to keep the sun out of his eyes, and looks. Love makes the eyesight very keen. He cannot recognize his boy by his rags, but he knows his son's very gait.

"That's my boy! That's my son! He's coming back!" he exclaims.

Downstairs he rushes, his gray hair flying in the wind; he has never been seen to go so fast for years. He leaps into the highway. The servants wonder to see him rushing to meet a stranger. God never allows us to get ahead of Him.

"Father, I've sinned," begins the prodigal. But the old man won't hear a word.

"Run quickly and get the best robe. You run and bring a new ring. You fetch the best pair of shoes. You go and kill the fatted calf. Send for the musicians. We are going to have music, and rejoice."

The whole house is in excitement.

What a picture that is of the love of God, and His joy over the return of a sinner! Come, reader, are you not ashamed to stay away from such a Father? Will you not say "I will" this moment, and turn your face homewards? God is waiting to welcome you.

I see the old man weeping tears of joy. In that home there is gladness. The boy is eating that sumptuous meal; he has not had as good a meal for many a year. It seems almost too good to be true. Picture the scene. While he is there he begins to weep; and his old father, who is weeping for joy, looks over to him and says:

"What are you weeping for?"

The boy says: "Well, father, I was thinking it would be an awful thing if I should leave you again, and go into a foreign country."

But if you sit down at God's feast, you will not want to go back into the devil's country again. He go back? He will never go back to the swine and the husks.

Oh, my friends, come home! God wants you. His heart is aching for you. I do not care what your past life has been. Upon the authority of God's Word I proclaim salvation to every sinner. "This man receiveth sinners, and eateth with them." Every sinner has a false idea of God; he thinks God is not ready and willing to forgive him. He says it is not justice. But God wants to deal in mercy. If the old father had dealt in justice, he would have barred the door and said to his son:

"You cannot come into my house."

That is not what fathers are doing. Their doors are not barred against their own children. Their doors are wide open, and they bid you come home. There is no father on earth who has as much love in his heart as God has for you. You may be black as hell; yet God stands ready and willing to receive you to His bosom, and to forgive you freely.

When I was preaching once in Philadelphia, a poor, fallen woman came into the meeting. The sermon did not touch her until I got to that part where I said: "There is no sinner so vile but Jesus will receive that one"; and it went like an arrow to her soul. She came to the inquiry room, and made up her mind never to go back. In the course of forty-eight hours she found her way to the feet of Jesus. Two Christian ladies went to see her mother; and when they came to her house, she was not going to let them in. She was sick and did not want to receive any callers; but the thought came to her that perhaps they were bringing good news from her husband. When these two angels of light came in, they said they came to talk about her daughter, Mary. The woman said:

"My daughter? have you brought news of my child? Where is she? Oh, how my heart has ached for fifteen long years. Why did you not bring her with you?"

They said: "We did not know that you would receive her."

She said: "Oh, how my heart has been aching! Won't you bring her back tomorrow morning?"

If the mother received that child, do you tell me God would not receive her? There is not a sinner on earth whom God will not receive if he repents.

William Dawson, the celebrated Yorkshire farmer, once said that there was no man so far gone in London that Christ would not receive him. A young lady called on him and said:

"I heard you say that there was no man so far gone in London that Christ would not receive him. Did you mean it?"

"Yes," he said.

"Well," she said, "I have found a man who says he is so bad that the Lord will not have anything to do with him. Will you go and see him?"

He said: "I will be glad to go."

She took him to a brick building in a narrow street; and he was in the fifth story. She said:

"You had better go in alone."

He went in and found a young man lying in the garret, on an old straw bed. He was very sick. Mr. Dawson whispered in his ear some kind words, and wanted to call his friends.

The dying man said: "You are mistaken in the person."

"Why so?" said Mr. Dawson.

"I have no friends on earth," said the dying man,

It is hard indeed, for a man to serve the devil, and come down to no friends.

"Well," said he, "you have a friend in Christ"; and he told him how Jesus loved and pitied him, and would save him, He read different portions of Scripture, and prayed with the man. After praying with him a long time, the light of the gospel began to break into his dark soul, and his heart went out towards those whom he had injured. He said:

"If my father would only forgive me, I could die happy."

"Who is your father?"

He told him, and Mr. Dawson said, "I will go and see him."

"No," the sick man said; "he has cast me off."

But William Dawson knew he would receive him, so he got his father's address and said:

"I will go."

He came to the west end of London, and rang the bell of the house where the father lived. A servant in livery came to the door, and Mr. Dawson asked if his master was in. The servant showed him in, and told him to wait a few minutes. Presently the merchant came in. Mr. Dawson said to him:

"You have a son by the name of Joseph."

The merchant said: "No sir; if you come to talk to me about that worthless vagabond, you shall leave the house. I have disinherited him."

Mr. Dawson said: "He will not be your boy by night; but he will be as long as he lives."

The man said, "Is my boy sick?"

"Yes, he is dying. I do not ask you to help bury him, I will attend to that; but he wants you to forgive him, and then he will die in peace."

The tears trickled down the father's cheeks. Said he: "Does Joseph want me to forgive him? I would have forgiven him long ago if I had known that."

In a few minutes he was in a carriage, and they went to the house where the boy was; and as they ascended the filthy stairs, he said:

"Did you find my boy here? I would have taken him to my heart if I had known this."

The boy cried, when his father came in: "Can you forgive me all my past sins?"

The father bent over him, and kissed him, and said: "I would have forgiven you long ago." And he added: "Let my servant put you in my carriage."

The dying man said: "I am too sick—I can die happy now. I think God, for Christ's sake, has forgiven me."

The prodigal told the father of the Savior's love; and then, his head lying upon his father's bosom, he breathed his last, and rose to heaven.

If your father or mother forsake you, the Lord Jesus Christ will not. Oh, press into the kingdom of heaven now. Come home!

Mr. Spurgeon once summed up the things his audience had got over. Some, he said, had got over the prayers of faithful Sabbath-school teachers who used to weep over them and come to the house and talk to them. They resisted all their entreaties, and got over their influence. And some had got over their mother's tears and prayers, and she, perhaps, sleeps in the grave today. Some had got over the tears and prayers of their father and of their minister, who had prayed with them and wept with them, a godly, faithful minister. There was a time when his sermons got right hold of them, but they have got over them now, and his sermons make no impression. Some had been through special meetings, and they have made no impression; they have not touched them. Still they say they are getting on. Well, so they are; but bear in mind, they are getting on as fast as they can to hell, and there is not one man in ten thousand who can hope to be saved after he has grown so hard-hearted.

Oh, reader, if you are not already a child of God, safe bound for the Father's home, or if you are a wandering child, off in the far country, say, "I will arise" now! Let there be joy in heaven today over your return.

THE PRODIGAL'S LOSSES | By HENRY MOORHOUSE

The fifteenth chapter of Luke is one which almost every one could repeat from memory, and yet it is one of those beautiful portions which always seem to touch one's heart and fill one's soul with fresh joy every time one reads it. I wish you to look at this sweet chapter in connection with the Christian life. We have commonly been accustomed to look at it in connection with the state of unsaved sinners, and there is no doubt that it may be applied to them. But I wish to draw another lesson from it, and apply it to our souls. I think I shall be justified in applying it to the Christian, as well as to the sinner who has never known the Father's house and the Father's love.

You remember that the people to whom the Lord Jesus Christ spoke this beautiful parable were all Jews.

A WORD FOR BACKSLIDERS.

The Jews had drifted away from God, and had become backsliders; and thus I can find a message to backsliders from this beautiful chapter. I do not know any place where the unsaved sinner is spoken of as the son of the Father.

In this story, the Lord Jesus Christ was surrounded by the publicans and sinners, while the Pharisees and scribes were in the distance, and began to murmur and find fault. You will always find that the Pharisees who keep away find fault, but the sinners who come near do not find fault at all. The faultfinders said:

"This man receiveth sinners, and eateth with them."

Then He spake this parable unto them,

"A certain man had two sons: and the younger of them said to his father, Father, give me the portion of goods that falleth to me.

"And he divided unto them his living. And not many days after, the younger son gathered all together, and took his journey into a far country, and there wasted his substance with riotous living. And when he had spent all, there arose a mighty famine in that land: and he began to be in want."

Now notice what kind of a famine it was. It was not a famine of husks—there were plenty of those. It was not a famine of swine's flesh—there was plenty of that. But there was a famine of that which was clean, and fit for a Jew to eat. There is never a famine of husks; the devil has not had a famine for the last nineteen hundred years. There are always plenty of husks to feed hungry swine, and there are always plenty of hungry swine to eat them. Go where you will, you will always find plenty of devil's food for hungry souls; but it will not satisfy.

Now the story goes on to say, that when the prodigal had wasted his substance, he went and joined himself to a citizen of that country, and asked him for something to do; and I do not for one moment believe that the citizen had the least pity for him. He saw the young man was a Jew, and he said:

"The only thing you are fit for is to go and feed my swine."

That was neither pity nor sympathy; it was a piece of mockery. Nothing pleases sinners so much as to see a child of God brought down to their level.

Now what did the prodigal lose? There was something that he could not lose, but there was much that he could.

In the first place, he could lose his home. His father's home was not closed against him, but in that far country, he had

NO HOME.

Some would say, "I would not be a prodigal. It must be something very terrible to disgrace my church, to give the devil my service in the eyes of the world, to get intoxicated and go reeling about the streets."

Yes, that is getting into the far country; but, beloved friend, I believe it is possible to be in the "far country," and, at the same time, be in attendance upon God's house and joining in its services. I believe it is possible to be in the "far country" while reading the blessed Book; to be in the "far country" with the wine and bread, which are emblems of the broken body of my Savior, in my hand. Nay, more; I believe it is possible to be in the "far country" while teaching about the prodigal son. Whenever we get our affections fixed upon earth, that is the "far country." The farthest from heaven that the Christian can get is the world; and, while we are living for the world, our heart is in the "far country." Beloved friend, we need not give up our seat in church, we need not give up church membership; only let our heart be away from Christ, and centered upon earth, and we are in the "far country."

Now see what he loses. Home! That sweet word! "Home! sweet home! there's no place like home!"

It is only those who have been in the far country who know what it is to love home.

MEMORIES OF HOME.

I remember when I was in California with a friend. We had come from Sacramento, and had been in the cars four hours. We had a short time to wait, and got out and walked about. We were enchanted with the beautiful scenery. The mountain tops, covered with snow, looked like masses of silver. My friend said he had been to Switzerland, and had seen nothing like it. There was a lake, and in the sunlight it looked like a sea of gold. We were admiring the scenery, when the birds began to warble, and a little blackbird began to sing. Before we knew what we were doing, we had forgotten the scenery, and tears were streaming down our faces. It was the first blackbird that we had heard sing in that country, and it seemed to be like the song of old England. Ah! "there's no place like home." The scenery may be grand, beautiful and glorious, but there is no place like home.

So, in the far country, the prodigal had lost his home. There was no familiar face to welcome him, and no kind voice to cheer him.

He had lost his home, and he had lost something else too; he had lost

HIS FOOD.

He had the husks, but they did not satisfy him. He lost his food; and I think the Church of God has lost her food, and that is the cause of the terrible state of weakness the Church is in. You cannot have food away from your Father's house. You must come back home; you will never be satisfied in the far country. What was the reason that the men of God had such power in the ancient days? Because they ate the bread that God sent them. Turn to the fourteenth chapter of Genesis, and you will find an illustration of what I mean. What did Abram say? He would not take so much as a thread or a shoe-latchet. Sodom was a wealthy city, but Abram would have none of her goods, and would only take the piece of bread and drink of wine from the priest of the Most High God. Why? He knew that the servant of the Most High God should be independent of Sodom; and when the Church of God finds out that, and acts upon it, it will be a grand thing.

But, though he refused the goods of Sodom, Abram took the bread and drank the wine that typified Christ; and those who take that food, will not want to get rich with the goods of Sodom.

Turn now to the eleventh chapter of Numbers, and there you will find another illustration:

"And the mixed multitude that was amongst them fell a lusting: and the children of Israel also wept again, and said, Who shall give us flesh to eat?"

The "mixed multitude"; they were those who came up out of Egypt with the children of Israel, but were not under the shelter of the blood of the Lamb. They were a hindrance to God's people. They said:

"We remember the fish which we did eat in Egypt freely, the cucumbers, and the melons, and the leeks, and the onions, and the garlic; but now there is nothing at all but this manna."

What was the manna? It was the God-given bread, which they began to tire of, remembering the fish, melons, cucumbers, onions, leeks and garlic. They remembered these things, but forgot the bondage, the groaning, the tears, the tale of bricks they had to make, and the whip of the taskmasters. The devil will readily enough remind you of the leeks, onions and garlic, but not of the bondage. The devil will tell you of anything except the true manna, which is Christ, and you cannot be fed unless fed by Him.

LOST WORK AND TESTIMONY.

The prodigal lost his food, but that was not all. He lost his work. He could not take care of his father's sheep while in the far country. His father's lambs might need tending, but he could not nurse them there; and his father's harvest might need gathering, but he could not do it there.

Beloved, you cannot work from your Father's home, for He will not ask any child to work until He has first fed him; we can neither feed nor work in the far country.

He had lost something else, also, and that was his testimony. He had a ragged coat on his back, and not a cent in his pocket, and who would believe him if he talked about his father? He might say his father was the richest man in Judea; but, with his ragged coat and penniless pocket, they would only laugh at him in the far country, and would not believe his testimony. Why do people not believe our testimony? Because we talk of a rich father, and yet go about with a ragged coat; we talk of joy, and look wretched; we talk of peace, and look full of trouble. That is why our testimony is not believed.

Then this is what the prodigal lost: his home, his food, his work and his testimony. But he did not lose all. It is one thing to go to heaven, and it is another to waste the only life that God ever gave for His service. What if the Mighty God of heaven were to summon around Him all the angels in glory, and He were to say:

"There is a mission going on in yonder town, and there are thousands of people in the back streets, and nobody is speaking to them about My beloved Son; no one is asking them to go to the hall to hear of salvation, I have hundreds of people in that town who never speak for Me."

I know some say they could die for Christ. But He does not want you to die for Him. He wants you to live for Him; to speak of His blood, and to weep over lost ones for Him. He would do it for *you*, but you would not do it for *Him*!

If the angels only had the privilege to leave that glorious place in heaven, and come down to win souls for Christ, how many would go? or rather, how many would stop behind? I do not believe a single angel would be left in heaven; they would so prize the privilege for which God's children on earth care so little.

But although the prodigal lost his home, food, work and testimony, he did not lose his sonship and he did not lose his citizenship. Once a man was a Jew, it was impossible to make him a Gentile. He did not lose his sonship either. That, too, is impossible. He may be disinherited, but he is a son all the same.

A FATHER'S LOVE.

When I was at home, in Manchester, our family consisted of two brothers and two sisters. My brother was a bad boy, a prodigal, and they could not get him to work in the mill.

One of my sisters said to her father, "Father, I will tell thee what thee ought to do with our John; turn him into the street."

"Why?" asked the father.

"Why," she said, "see how good we all are, and how bad he is; he is a disgrace to us. Turn him away."

Christmas Day came, and the family was together, and the old man read a chapter and prayed, and the prodigal was present. The father, turning around to the daughter, said:

"Well, what are we to do with thy brother now?"

Her reply was, "Put him in the street."

Then he turned, put the question to a friend, and he said he did not like to interfere, but he thought it would do him good to turn him out a little. The old man left his chair, and said: "John, thy sister and brother and friend say I should turn thee out; but I am thy poor old father, and I will never put thee in the street, my boy."

The prodigal was overcome by the father's love: It was the means of leading his heart to the Lord, and he is now a preacher of the Gospel.

NEVER TOO LATE.

Oh, if you are in the far country, if all the angels in heaven turn their backs upon you, if all the devils in hell tell you you cannot be saved, and if your own heart says it is too late, never mind them—go home! Go back in spite of earth and hell, and tell your Father how you have wandered, and He will receive you; for the door is never shut, and a son will ever find a welcome. The prodigal went back, but it was with a downcast face: he did not see his father, but his father saw him, and he ran to meet him. This is the only place where we read of God being in a hurry. He did not run to create a world, but He ran to put His arms around the neck of a poor prodigal. Oh, never, *never*, NEVER doubt your Heavenly Father's love! If you have wandered, go back and tell Him your sin, and He will receive you with a kiss upon your lips.

And when the prodigal went home, he found the fatted calf ready. The fatted calf is always ready, do not doubt!

THE IRISH MOTHER'S BOY.

Once I was at Dublin, and a lady of the Society of Friends said to me,

"Henry Moorhouse, I want thee to go and speak to a poor woman who is in great trouble."

I went and found the poor old woman in her cottage in a sad state, rocking herself to and fro, and moaning.

I asked her what troubled her, and she said her boy had broken her heart. She said:

"You know my boy has gone away, and I had a letter from him today, and that has nearly broken my heart."

She read me the letter, and she came to the words, "Dear mother, if you can never forgive me, don't curse me."

Then she broke out again, "I never knew how much I loved him until he went away, and now to think he should say, 'Mother, don't curse me.'"

It was the doubt of the mother's love that broke her heart.

Oh, when any one can doubt our Heavenly Father's love, they must be in the far country! Come back, brother; come back, sister; come back today! The door is open, and there stands the loving Father. Say to Him, "I will arise, and go home." That moment the Father's arms will be around your neck. Come, *come*, COME! Come to thy loving Father's arms, come back to thy home, come back to thy God, come back to thy work, come back *now!*

THE PRODIGAL'S CLIMAX | By C. H. SPURGEON

There are different stages in the sinner's history, and they are worth marking in the prodigal's experience. There is, first, the stage in which the young man sought independence of his father. The younger son said:

'Father, give me the portion of goods that falleth to me."

We know something of that state of mind; and, alas! it is a very common one. As yet there is no open profligacy, no distinct rebellion against God. Religious services are attended, the father's God is held in reverence; but in his heart the young man desires a supposed liberty, he wishes to cast off all restraint. Companions hint that he is too much tied to his mother's apron-string. He himself feels that there may be some strange delights which he has never enjoyed; and the curiosity of Mother Eve to taste the fruit of that tree which was good for food and pleasant to the eyes and a tree to be desired to make one wise, comes into the young man's mind, and he wishes to put forth his hand and take the fruit of the tree of the knowledge of good and evil, that he may eat thereof. He never intends to spend his substance in riotous living, but he would like to have the opportunity of spending it as he likes. He does not mean to be a profligate; still, he would like to have the honor of choosing what is right on his own account.

At any rate, he is a man now; he feels his blushing honors full upon him, and he wants now to exercise his own freedom of will, and to feel that he himself is really his own master. Who, indeed, he asks, is lord over him? Perhaps there are some reading this who are just in such a state as that; if so, may the grace of God arrest you before you go any further away from Him! May you feel that to be out of gear with God, to wish to be separated from Him, and to have other interests than those of Him who made you, must be dangerous, and probably will be fatal! Therefore now, even now, may you come to yourself at this earliest stage of your history, and also come to love and rejoice in God as the prodigal returned to his father!

Very soon, however, this young man in the parable entered upon quite another stage. He had received his portion of goods; all that he would have had at his father's death he had turned into ready money, and there it is. It is his own, and he may do what he pleases with it. Having already indulged his independent feeling towards his father, and his wish to have a separate establishment altogether from him, he knew that he would be freer to carry out his plans if he was right away. Anywhere near his father there is a check upon him; he feels that the influence of his home somewhat clips his wings. If he could get into a far country, there he should have the opportunity to develop; and all that evolution could do for him he would have the opportunity of enjoying. So he gathers all together, and goes into the far country.

It may be that I am addressing some who have reached that stage. Now there is all the delirium of self-indulgence. Now it is all gaiety, "a short life and a merry one," forgetting the long eternity and a woeful one. Now the cup is full, and the red wine sparkles in the bowl. As yet, it has not bitten you like a serpent, nor stung you like an adder, as it will do all too soon; but just now, it is the deadly sweetness that you taste, and the exhilaration of that drugged chalice that deceives you. You are making haste to enjoy yourself. Sin is a dangerous joy, beloved all the more because of the danger; for where there is a fearful risk, there is often an intense pleasure to a daring heart; and you perhaps are one of that venturous band, spending your days in folly and your nights in riotousness.

Ere long there comes a third stage to the sinner as well as to the prodigal, that is when he has "spent all."

We have only a certain amount of spending money after all. He who has gold without limit, yet has not health without limit; or if health does not fail him in his sinning, yet desire fails, and satiety comes in, as it did with Solomon when he tried this way of seeking happiness. At last, there is no honey left, there is only the sting of the bee. At last, there is no sweetness in the cup, there is only the delirium that follows the intoxication. At last, the meat is eaten to the bone, and there is nothing good to come out of that bone; it contains no marrow; the teeth are broken with it; and the man wishes that he had never sat down to so terrible a feast. He has reached the stage at which the prodigal arrived when he had spent all.

Oh, there be some who spend all their character, spend all their health and strength, spend all their hope, spend all their uprightness, spend everything that was worth having! They have spent all. This is another stage in the sinner's history, and it is very apt to lead to despair, and even deeper sin, and sometimes to that worst of sins which drives a man red-handed before the face of his Maker to account for his own blood.

It is a dreadful state to be in, for there comes at the back of it a terrible hunger. There is a weary labor to get something that may stay the spirit, a descending to the degradation of feeding swine, a willingness to eat of the husks that swine do eat, yet an inability to do so. Many have felt this craving that cannot be satisfied. But, for my part, I am glad when "the rake's progress" has reached this point; for often, in the grace of God, it is the way home for the prodigal; it is a roundabout way, but it is the way home for him. When men have spent all, and poverty has followed on their recklessness, and sickness has come at the call of their vice, then it is that omnipotent grace has stepped in, and there has come another stage in the sinner's history, of which I am now going to speak, as God may help me. That is the point the prodigal had reached when he came to himself."

I. Then, first

A SINNER IS BESIDE HIMSELF.

While he is living in his sin he is out of his mind, he is beside himself. I am sure that it is so. There is nothing more like to madness than sin; and it is a moot point among those who study deep problems how far insanity and the tendency to sin go side by side, and whereabouts it is that great sin and entire loss of responsibility may touch each other. I do not intend to discuss that question at all; but I am going to say that every sinner is morally and responsibly insane, and therefore in a worse condition than if he were only mentally insane.

He is insane, first, because *his judgment is altogether out of order*. He makes fatal mistakes about all-important matters. He reckons a short time of this mortal life to be worth all his thoughts, and he puts eternity into the background. He considers it possible for a creature to be at enmity against the Creator, or indifferent to Him, and yet to be happy. He fancies that he knows better what is right for him than the law of God declares. He dreams that the everlasting gospel, which cost God the life of His own Son, is scarcely worthy of his attention at all, and he passes it by with contempt. He has unshipped the rudder of his judgment, and steers towards the rocks with awful deliberation, and seems as if he would wish to know where he can find the surest place to commit eternal shipwreck. His judgment is out of order.

Further, *his actions are those of a madman.* This prodigal son, first of all, had interests apart from his father. He must have been mad to have conceived such an idea as that. For me to have interests apart from Him who made me, and keeps me alive—for me, the creature of an hour, to fancy that I can have a will in opposition to the will of God, and that I can so live and prosper—why, I must be a fool! I must be mad to wish any such thing, for it is consistent with the highest reason to believe that he who yields himself up to omnipotent goodness must be in the track of happiness, but that he who sets himself against the almighty grace of God must certainly be kicking against the pricks to his own wounding and hurt. Yet this sinner does not see that it is so, and the reason is that he is beside himself.

Then, next, that young man went away from his home, though it was the best home in all the world. We can judge that from the exceeding tenderness and generosity of the father at the head of it, and from the wonderful way in which all the servants had such entire sympathy with their master. It was a happy home, well stored with all that the son could need; yet he quits it to go, he knows not whither, among strangers who did not care a straw for him, and who, when they had drained his purse, would not give him even a cent with which to buy bread to save him from starving. The prodigal must have been mad to act like that; and for any of us to leave Him who has been the dwelling-place of His saints in all generations, to quit the warmth and comfort of the Church of God which is the home of joy and peace, is clear insanity. Anyone who does this is acting against his own best interests, he is choosing the path of shame and sorrow, he is casting away all true delight; he must be mad.

You can see further that this young man is out of his mind, because, when he gets into the far country, he begins spending his money riotously. He does not lay it out judiciously. He spends his money for that which is not bread, and his labor for that which satisfieth not; and that is just what the sinner does. If he be self-righteous, he is trying to weave a robe out of the worthless material of his own works; and if he be a voluptuary, given up to sinful indulgences, what vanity it is for him to hope for pleasure in the midst of sin! Should I expect to meet with angels in the sewers, with heavenly light in a dark mine? Nay, these are not places for such things; and can I rationally look for joy to my heart from reveling, chambering, wantonness, and such conduct? If I do, I must be mad. Oh, if men were but rational—and they often wrongly suppose that they are—if they were but rational beings, they would see

HOW IRRATIONAL IT IS TO SIN!

The most reasonable thing in the world is to spend life for its own true design, and not to fling it away as though it were a pebble on the sea-shore.

Further, the prodigal was a fool, he was mad, for he spent all. He did not even stop half way on the road to penury, but he went on till he had spent all.

There is no limit to those who have started on a course of sin. He that stays back from it, by God's grace may keep from it; but it is with sin as it is with the intoxicating cup.

One said to me: "I can drink much, or I can drink none; but I have not the power to drink a little, for if I begin I cannot stop myself, and may go to any length."

So it is with sin. God's grace can keep you abstaining from sin; but, if you begin sinning, oh, how one sin draws on another! One sin is the decoy or magnet for another sin, and draws you on; and one cannot tell, when he begins to descend this slippery slide, how quickly and how far he may go. Thus the prodigal spent all in utter recklessness; and, oh, the recklessness of some young sinners whom I know! And, oh, the greater recklessness of some old sinners who seem resolved to be damned, for, having but a little remnant of life left, they waste that last fragment of it in fatal delay.

Then it was, dear friends, when the prodigal had spent all, that he still further proved his madness. That would have been the time to go home to his father; but, apparently, that thought did not occur to him. "He went and joined himself to a citizen of that country," still overpowered by the fascination that kept him away from the one place where he might have been happy; and that is one of the worst proofs of the madness of some who, though they know about the great God and His infinite mercy, and know somewhat of how much they need Him and His grace, yet still they try to get what they want somewhere else and do not go back to Him.

The prodigal had the ways of a madman. I have had, at times, to deal with those whose reason has failed them, and I have noticed that many of them have been perfectly sane, and even wise and clever, on all points except one. So it is with the sinner. He is a famous politician; just hear him talk. He is a wonderful man of business; see how sharply he looks after every cent. He is very judicious in everything but this, he is mad on one point, he has a fatal monomania, for it concerns his own soul.

Mad people do not know that they have been mad till they are cured; they think that they alone are wise, and all the rest are fools. Here is another point of their resemblance to sinners, for they also think that everybody is wrong except themselves. Hear how they will abuse a pious wife as "a fool." What hard words they will use towards a gracious daughter! How they will rail at the ministers of the gospel, and try to tear God's Bible to pieces! Poor mad souls, they think all are mad except themselves! We, with tears, pray God to deliver them from their delusions, and to bring them to sit at the feet of Jesus, clothed and in their right minds.

II. Secondly,

IT IS A BLESSED THING WHEN THE SINNER COMES TO HIMSELF.

"When he came to himself." This is the first mark of grace working in the sinner as it was the first sign of hope for the prodigal.

It appears that when the prodigal came to himself he was shut up to two thoughts. Two facts were clear to him—that there was plenty in his father's house, and that he himself was famishing. May the two kindred spiritual facts have absolute power over your heart, if you are yet unsaved; for they were most certainly all important and pressing truths.

If we could shut up unconverted men to those two thoughts, what hopeful congregations we should have.

This change is often sudden. There came into the Metropolitan Tabernacle one morning a man who had not for a long time gone to any place of worship. He despised such things; he could swear, and drink, and do worse things still; he was careless, godless; but he had a mother who often prayed for him, and he had a brother whose prayer has never ceased for him. He did not come to worship, he came just to see the preacher whom his brother had been hearing for so many years; but, coming in, somehow he was no sooner in the place than he felt that he was unfit to be there, so he went up into the top gallery, as far back as he could, and when some friend beckoned him to take a seat, he felt that he could not do so, he must just lean against the wall at the back. Someone else invited him to sit down, but he could not; he felt that he had no right to do so.

The preacher announced his text,—"And the publican, standing afar off, would not lift up so much as his eyes unto heaven, but smote upon his breast, saying, God be merciful to me a sinner";—and said something like this, "You that stand farthest off in the Tabernacle, and dare not sit down because you feel your guilt to be so great, you are the man to whom God has sent me this morning, and he bids you come to Christ and find mercy."

A miracle of love was then wrought. He came to himself. I rejoiced greatly when I heard of it, for in his case there was a change that everybody who knew him could see. He became full of a desire after everything that is gracious as once he practiced everything that was bad. Now that is what sometimes happens, and why should it not happen again this moment? Why should not some other man or woman come to himself or to herself now? This is the way home, first to come to yourself, and then to come to your God. "He came to himself."

Now let us consider *how this change happened.* If you should ask me the outward circumstances of the prodigal's case, I should say that it took a great deal to bring him to himself.

"Why, surely!" one says, "he ought to have come to himself when he had spent all. He must have come to himself when he began to be hungry."

No; it took a great deal to bring him to himself and to his father; and it takes a great deal to bring sinners to themselves and to their God. There are some of you who will have to be beaten with many stripes before you will be saved. I heard one say, who was crushed almost to death in an accident,

"If I had not nearly perished, I should have wholly perished."

So is it with many sinners; if some had not lost all they had, they would have lost all; but, by strong winds, rough and raging, some are driven into the port of peace.

THE OCCASION OF THE PRODIGAL'S CLIMAX,

of his coming to himself, was this; he was very hungry and in great sorrow, and he was alone. It is a grand thing if we can get people to be alone. There was nobody near the poor man, and no sound for him to hear except the grunting of the hogs, and the munching of those husks. Ah, to be alone! It is a good thing for a sinner sometimes to be alone. The prodigal had nobody to drink with him, nobody to sport with him; he was too far gone for that. He had not a rag to pawn to get another pint, he must therefore just sit still without one of his old companions. They only followed him for what they could get out of him. As long as he could treat them, they would treat him well; but when he had spent all, "no man gave unto him." He was left without a comrade, in misery he could not allay, in hunger he could not satisfy. He pulled that belt up another hole, and made it tighter; but it almost seemed as if he would pull himself in two if he drew it any closer. He was reduced almost to a skeleton; emaciation had taken hold of him, and he was ready to lie down there and die. Then it was that he came to himself.

Do you know why *this change occurred in the prodigal's case*? I believe that the real reason was that his father was secretly working for him all the while. His state was known to his father; I am sure it was, because the elder brother knew it; and if the elder brother heard of it, so did the father. The elder brother may have told him; or, if not, the father's greater love would have a readier ear for tidings of his son than the elder brother had.

Perhaps somebody says, "I wish I could come to myself, sir, without going through all that process."

Well, you have come to yourself already if you really wish that. Let me suggest to you that, in order to prove that it is so, you should begin seriously to think, to think about who you are, and where you are, and what is to become of you. Take time to think, and think in an orderly, steady, serious manner; and, if you can, jot down your thoughts. It is a wonderful help to some people to put down upon paper an account of their own condition. I believe that there were many who found the Savior one night when I urged them, when they went home, to write on a piece of paper, "Saved as a believer in Jesus," or else, "Condemned because I believe not on the Son of God." Some who began to write that word "condemned" have never finished it, for they found Christ there and then while seeking Him.

You keep your account books, do you not? I am sure you do if you are in trade, unless you are going to cheat your creditors. You keep your business books; well, now,

KEEP A RECORD CONCERNING YOUR SOUL.

Really look these matters in the face—the hereafter, death which may come so suddenly, the great eternity, the judgment-seat. Do think about these things; do not shut your eyes to them. Men and women, I pray you, do not play the fool! If you must play the fool, take some lighter things to trifle with than your souls and your eternal destinies. Shut yourselves up alone for a while; go through this matter steadily, lay it out in order, make a plan of it. See where you are going. Think over the way of salvation, the story of the cross, the love of God, the readiness of Christ to save; and I think that while this process is going on, you will feel your heart melting, and soon you will find your soul believing in the precious blood which sets the sinner free.

WHEN HE CAME TO HIMSELF, THEN HE CAME TO HIS FATHER.

When a sinner comes to himself, he soon comes to his God. This poor prodigal, soon after he came to himself, said,

"I will arise, and go to my father."

What led him back to his father? Very briefly let me answer that question.

First, *his memory aroused him.* He recollected his father's house, he remembered the past, his own riotous living.

Do not try to forget all that has happened; the terrible recollections of a misspent past may be the means of leading you to a new life. Set memory to work.

Next, *his misery bestirred him.* Every pang of hunger that he felt, the sight of his rags, the degradation of associating with swine—all those things drove him back to his father.

O, reader, let your very needs, your cravings, your misery, drive you to your God!

Then, *his fears whipped him back.* He said, "I perish with hunger." He had not perished yet, but he was afraid that he soon would do so; he feared that he really would die, for he felt so faint.

O, reader, see what will become of you if you do die in your sins! What awaits you but an endless future of limitless misery? Sin will follow you into eternity, and will increase upon you there, and as you shall go on to sin, so shall you go on to sorrow ever-increasing. A deeper degradation and a more tremendous penalty will accompany your sin in the world to come; therefore let your fears drive you home, as they drove home the poor prodigal.

Meanwhile, *his hope drew him*. This gentle cord was as powerful as the heavy whip:

"In my father's house there is bread enough and to spare; I need not perish with hunger, I may yet be filled."

Oh, think of what you may yet be! Poor sinner, think of what God can do and is ready to do for you, to do for you even now! How happy He can make you! How peaceful and how blessed! So let your hope draw you to Him.

Then, *his resolve moved him*. He said, "I will arise and go to my father." All else drove him or drew him and now he is resolved to return home. He rose up from the earth on which he had been sitting amidst his filthiness, and he said,

"I will."

Then the man became a man. He had come to himself; the manhood had come back to him, and he said, "I will, I will."

Lastly, there was *the real act of going to his father*; it was that which brought him home. Nay, let me correct myself; it is said, *"He came to his father,"* but there is a higher truth at the back of that, for *his father came to him*.

So, when you are moved to return, and the resolution becomes an action, and you arise, and go to God, salvation is yours almost before you could have expected it; for, once turn your face that way, and while you are yet a great way off, your Father will outstrip the wind, and come and meet you, and fall upon your neck, and kiss you with the kisses of reconciliation.

This shall be your portion if you will but trust the Lord Jesus Christ.

"HE CAME TO HIMSELF" | By W. HAY HITKEN

"And when he came to himself." —Luke XV, 17.

Here the sinner is presented to us as suffering from a species of moral insanity.

I was once conducting a mission in the north of England, and the clergyman in whose church I was preaching, received from an anonymous correspondent one of the handbills which had been circulated in preparation for the mission, with two words added after the words, "A mission"—viz.: "for lunatics," so that it read, "A mission for lunatics!" I do not suppose that the man who wrote those words had any particular intention of telling the truth, but it is startling to think how near the truth he came.

Perhaps, if we could see things as those bright intelligences see them, who are permitted to hover round this world of ours, and to be witnesses of human action, we should be disposed to regard this world of ours as one great lunatic asylum. It must seem strange to them that to men and women there should be made such glorious offers, that before their eyes there should be spread such magnificent possibilities, and that in the folly of their unbelief they should turn their back upon their own truest interest, and sin against their own souls.

Lunatics, indeed! There are *dangerous lunatics*, frenzied by passion or goaded by ambition, so dangerous that sometimes their fellow-lunatics have to put a kind of restraint upon them, for fear that the paroxysms of their moral disease should injure society too seriously.

Then there are *harmless lunatics*, men and women whose lives are simply insipid, who seem to be just as void of any object in life as the butterfly that flits from flower to flower, drifted about by every influence that happens to be for the moment affecting them, without any recognition of the dignity of their own being.

Then again, there are the *self-complacent lunatics*, the men and women who are so particularly self-satisfied that they can afford to look down upon everybody else, and persuade themselves that they are models of good sense, and that those who are possessed of that spiritual wisdom which comes from above, are themselves in a state of insanity.

Is it not so? Is not that just the way in which self-complacent men of the world speak about those who know something about the realities of eternity? Have we not heard it again and again, till we are almost tired of hearing it, ever since the days when Festus charged Paul with being "beside himself"? Did not that man who wrote those two words on that handbill just mean that he, in his own self-complacency, was so satisfied with his own good sense that he regarded those who believed in eternity and accordingly began to make preparation for it, as little better than fools?

Indeed, this is one of the features of lunacy. Go into a lunatic asylum, and you will always find a large number of patients who regard themselves as injured persons, who are suffering not from their own disease of insanity, but from the insanity of other people. There are some who fancy themselves kings upon their thrones, and their subjects too insane to render them the honor which is their due. Others who imagine themselves men of vast wealth and possessions, and those who ought to be their servants too insane to render them the service they have a rightful claim to. So, while they persuade themselves that they are indeed in the full possession of their senses, they also contrive to please themselves by thinking that other persons who are actually sane, are afflicted with the very disease from which they are suffering.

Friends, it is even so in the spiritual world. The men and women whom Satan has deluded most completely, are just those who are the least conscious of their own insanity. The disease has taken so firm a hold upon their moral system that they believe that they are more sane than those who are living in the light of Divine wisdom. Their view of the case is an exact inversion of the truth; and as long as this moral infatuation continues, the efforts which are made by those who see things as they are, to awaken them from their fatal slumber, are regarded by these spiritual lunatics as simply the indication of mental obliquity, while they themselves, forsooth, in their profound stupor flatter themselves that they alone are reasonable beings.

Now this young man brought before us in this story is just the sort of person whom the world would describe as a *thoroughly sensible fellow*, I feel sure that such a man in our own day would be thus described by his companions. He showed his sense just in the way in which men of the world show theirs now. Let us regard him, for a few moments, from this point of view.

The first thing that this "sensible" man does is to feel

DISSATISFIED

within himself at the condition of dependence in which he is introduced to us. The father seems to have been in comfortable circumstances—perhaps in affluence, The young man has never been begrudged anything. All his wants have been supplied as fast as they have arisen. But then his position was one of dependence, and it was that that made things so far from agreeable. It was his father's way not to make him a regular allowance with which he might do as he liked, but to keep him constantly dependent upon him, from day to day, as his wants arose. He stinted him in nothing; but then it would have been so much pleasanter if the man had been allowed to take those means (which were employed indeed in his behalf), and use them himself as he liked. It was so humiliating to be dependent upon his father for everything. That this was the way in which the father treated the son, is evident from the statement of the elder brother. He says,

"Lo, these many years do I serve thee, and yet thou never gavest me a kid that I might make merry with my friends."

It was not his father's way to bestow his wealth upon his children, so that they might possess an independent property, but to supply their reasonable wants as fast as they occurred, and it was against this state of things that the man's will began to rebel.

"Why should not I be like other fellows? What a humiliating thing it is that I should be treated like a grownup child! If I had my own fortune, to do what I liked with, I should very soon be able to show this father of mine what the use of money is, and how it should be spent. Here I am, dependent upon him for everything. I cannot stand it any longer."

And so, like a thoroughly sensible man, he goes to his father and makes his plea:

"Father, give me the portion of goods that appertain to me. Why should I be kept in this condition any longer? I am of age, and surely I can judge for myself how my money should be spent. This property of yours is to belong to us one day. I may as well have my share now, to do what I like with."

The father does not refuse; he will not keep his son in a state of compulsory dependence upon him. There and then "he divided unto them his living." Observe, he divides his living between both his sons. It does not say that he gave half to the younger son and kept the other half himself, but "he divided unto them his living."

What became of the elder son's portion? Where did he invest it? How did he employ it? We find that long years afterwards this elder son says, "Thou never gavest me a kid that I might make merry with my friends." Ah! the elder brother had the wisdom to give back what was his. No sooner was his portion of goods assigned to him than he put it back again in safe keeping.

I can fancy him saying to his father, "I do not want my portion. I am quite happy. I have all I want."

In a moment of discontent, at a later period, he allows himself to speak hardly of his father's treatment, but this eldest son understood his father on the whole, although for a moment he might be unfaithful to the consciousness of the benefits of his position; and so he had the wisdom to give back what his father had given to him.

"I do not want it. I am perfectly contented. I have all that I desire. You have never grudged me anything. If I want anything I can always come to you for it. You and I are one. We are united together, and it is far pleasanter for me to know that all my life is in your hands, than for me to have the responsibility of keeping it myself. I might make mistakes: you have had far more experience than I, and you are far more likely to conserve my property, and to further my wellbeing, than I should be myself."

But the younger son was a far more sensible fellow than that, so as soon as he gets his money, he makes up his mind to spend it according to his own heart's desire. Thus the second thing this particularly sensible young man does, is to make up his mind that

THE RESTRAINTS OF HOME

are positively intolerable. He cannot go on in this droning way any longer. He must see something of the world. Life is hardly worth having under such conditions. He must break away from the restraints of the paternal roof, turn his back upon his old associations, and go forth and enjoy himself. He has had enough of this humdrum, tedious life. So like a very sensible young man, he leaves his father's home, and goes forth into a distant land.

I can fancy it costs him something at the moment. Nobody ever goes to hell without meeting with difficulties in the way. As he looks into his father's face and sees the tear rising in the old man's eye—as he takes a long last look at the dear old home where he had spent so many happy innocent years, I can fancy it costs him something. A better instinct would sometimes assert itself within his nature.

"Have you not been happy? Those sunny hours of childhood, what could have been more pleasant? If you have been unhappy it has been your own fault. If you had only availed yourself of all the opportunities of your position, you might have been as happy as any man need be. Your brother is a happy man; why should not you have been?"

But the lower instinct prevailed. His *downright good common-sense* was stronger than anything else; so that this thoroughly sensible man makes up his mind to turn his back upon his father's house, and into a distant land he goes.

Now, dear friends, before we follow him further, let us just compare his case with ours. Wherein does our good sense consist? How do the sensible men of our own day emulate the conduct of this person whose history is brought before us here? I reply, they act in precisely the same way.

The first thing the sinner desires to do is to assert his own independence. Our God does not deny us things that are suitable for us. It was a slander of Satan that suggested that God forbade our first parents to eat of the fruit of the trees of the garden. But God does desire us to take all that we have straight from His own hand, to live a life of continual dependence upon Him, to draw all our joy from Him, to be happy because we live in His society, and to find a blessed liberty in being continually His servants. This is the life God would have us live. Why? Because He is a tyrant? No; because He is a Friend. How does He show His friendliness by imposing such restraints upon us? Because He knows that His service is perfect freedom, and that it is only as we yield ourselves up to His service that we really can be partakers of the fulness of joy which it is His will that we should command.

Some *sensible men* don't think so. They have made up their mind that no greater evil can be apprehended than dependence. What is the root-sin of humanity? The turning aside of the human heart from its God. "I will not have God to reign over me. I will not be dictated to by His will. I will take my own way. I will run after my own desire. I will work out the counsels of my own heart. Self shall be my ruler, not Jehovah." This is

THE PRIME ACT OF REBELLION

which severs at once between the heart of man and his God, and prepares him for taking the second step which leads him out of the Divine presence into the distant country.

Are there not some of my readers who know in their own hearts that this has been the sin of their life-time? Brethren, have you been leading lives of dependence upon God? This is a plain question, is it not? Answer it. Have you taken your daily bread as coming from His hand? The pleasures of life—have you regarded them as the gift of His love? Life's friendships, life's joys, life's privileges—have they all been so many manifestations of His fatherly care? Has everything turned you Godward? In the midst of all the long battle of life have you been supported by a blessed sense of confidence in Him?

How many of you know that your experience has been just the opposite of all this: self-assertion, self-pleasing, running after your own desires, and gratifying your own passions—it is thus that you have lived. And such a life, what is it, dear friends? The world points to it and says it is the life of a sensible man. The angels point to it, and methinks, if we could hear their testimony, we should catch the word upon their lips, "It is the life of a lunatic, possessed of an evil spirit, who has blinded his understanding so that the man is utterly given over to strong delusion, and is utterly deaf to the voice of his own interests as well as to the commands of God."

Then, what next? Having asserted our own independence, the next thing is to get as far away from God as possible. We go into distant land; we do not want to have God in our thoughts. It is a disagreeable thing to hear God spoken about. Even in His holy house God is kept at a distance. We join in the service, but it is the music we are thinking of, not of God. We listen to the sermon, but it may be the eloquence of the preacher that we are attracted to, not the voice of God that we hear. We do not want to have anything to do with God; we keep Him as far away from us as possible. Why? Because we have gone into the far country.

This young man might have gone somewhere near home and enjoyed himself there, but he would not have been so comfortable as long as his father was near. He would not have liked his father's eye to follow him; he wanted to get away from all restraint; and the mere sight of his father's countenance would have been enough to mar his pleasure. So he goes into "the far country."

O, my friend, if, in the midst of the life of frivolity and sin which you are leading, you were suddenly brought face to face with God, what a pang of agony, what a thrill of terror would pass through you! How it would mar all your enjoyment and take away all comfort out of your life! You do not want to have anything to do with God. The less you have to do with Him the better. "The fool hath said in his heart, No God." "Let me take my own way; do not let Him interfere with my life." So it is that we go into the far country.

Cain went forth from the presence of God. He went into the land of wandering. He found plenty to occupy him there, but no God was there. Whatever else he had, the presence of God was excluded from his experience. He built him cities. He and his family made discoveries. They got on in the world, they multiplied, they prospered. Everything seemed to go well with them; and yet God was banished from their eyes, and their whole lives seemed to be designed to demonstrate how well man can get along without God. And the end of it all was, the flood came and destroyed them all.

Now what was the next step that this sensible fellow took? When he had asserted his independence and had got away from his father and the restraints of home, he began to enjoy himself. He "wasted his substance with riotous living." That does not sound very sensible just at first, but there are plenty of young men who show their good sense by pursuing the same course.

"Oh," you say, "we do not approve of fellows being spendthrifts." Yet you approve of men spending something that is

FAR MORE PRECIOUS THAN MONEY.

How have you been spending your *time*? What have you to show for it? How have you been spending your *influence*? You might have been using it for eternity, and already there might have been a crown of glory laid up as the result of well-used influence. What has become of it?

How have you been spending your money? for we may as well speak of that too. Some of you have been scattering it to the winds; others hoarding it up in the bank; some, laying it out in business speculations, and the very gold that you might have so used as to lay up for yourselves treasures in heaven, has become the curse of your life. How does it appear in God's sight? Wasted!—that substance of yours squandered, because it has never been turned to any really good purpose.

What about your *faculties and powers*,—your understanding, your affection, your will? All these things are so much treasure that has been put into your hand. You have asserted your own independence. You proclaim yourself master of all you possess. What have you done with it all? Just what this sensible man did. What results have you to show for all your expenditure? You have been lavish and profuse; has it brought you heart peace, deep inward satisfaction, calm, undying delight, the prospect of glory beyond the grave? What have you got by it? O, ye men of the world, who have lived so industriously for Satan, and wrought his will so unweariedly, what wages has he paid you? Are they not already beginning to overshadow your nature, withering up your faculties to a greater or lesser extent,—blighting your purer and holier desires,—dragging you down into a gaping sepulcher,—winding in your grave clothes, and preparing you as a wasted corpse for the burial of eternity, while you look sorrowfully upon the lost opportunities and the misspent energies of a wasted life.

What was the next thing that this sensible young man did? He formed a great many

GAY ACQUAINTANCES.

I do not think there is a young man that lives for the world but will agree that he shewed himself to be a "sensible" man in doing that. It is just what you do. How many a young man there is that is kept back from doing what he knows is right because he has formed so many acquaintances, and is surrounded by the influence of his companions? He would like to be different, but then he cannot shake off their influence; they keep him spell-bound. How "sensible" you are to let those friends of yours do the very worst that your worst enemy could desire to do for you! Do you think that really *is* "sensible"?

Take a good look at this picture. Does this young man, after all, seem a particularly sensible being? What are his friends doing for him? Well, they are kindly helping him to get rid of his money. He has got too much of it, and they are trying to help him squander it. If there is a feast, if there is a scene of debauchery, a wild revel, he has only to hold up his finger and he can get as many friends as he likes. What does he gain from them? He is giving a great deal away for their sakes; how much is he getting in exchange? Real friendship? You do not mean to say that is friendship;—that poor, empty, hollow masquerade, do you call that *friendship*? Do these friends stand by him for one moment in the practical battle of life? What has become of them when sickness smites the body, or disaster effects the purse, when prospects are blighted, and hopes are dashed? What becomes of your fine friends then? How readily they find it convenient to cut you in the street! With cold, pitiless scorn, they pass by those who are stricken on life's battle-field. You do not mean to say that you have carried your "sense" so far as to persuade yourselves that this is friendship?

I suppose this sensible man was flattering himself, in the midst of his revelry and folly, with the consideration:

"Well, I have a splendid retinue of friends around me. There is not a more popular man in the neighborhood. Look where I will, friendly eyes meet mine, friendly voices respond to my smile. I am a most fortunate fellow to make such friends as these."

Perhaps he thought so. Yet I cannot help thinking that in his graver moments he must have had misgivings. By and by there comes a change in his circumstances. Somehow or other, by their help or otherwise, his wealth has been got rid of, and he finds himself, for the first time in his life, alone. Where have they gone, those friends who swarmed around him? What has become of their blandishments? How is it that their smiles have forsaken their countenances? They seem to look at him coldly now. There is a distant salutation. By and by there is no salutation at all, and in that distant famine-stricken land he begins to find himself alone!

So will it be, dear friends, in the practical experience of life. Whether you take the path of outward sinner or not, and plunge into profligacy and vice, or whether your sins are of a more "respectable" nature, you will find plenty of people to back you in them. The opinion of society will be with you. The spirit of the world will stand by you valiantly until the critical moment comes. Let sorrow blight your heart, what about your worldly friends then? Let the blinds fall in your house, what consolation can they offer? Let disaster come, how can they help you? Let that body of yours be stricken with disease, what comfort can they administer? Let death approach, they fly in terror. O paltry, miserable friendship, can you do nothing more than this? Is it for such a friendship as this that men will turn their back upon their heavenly Father's house, and forfeit the present enjoyment of their Father's love, and participation in their Father's everlasting joy?

What was the next thing that this sensible young man did? When his pleasures had all failed him, when his roses had become thorns, then he began to be sober, and, like many sober people, began to look about for employment. He finds it rather difficult to obtain any employment that suits him. But employment he must have.

O! how like many of our worldly prodigals! when they have spent their youth in following one wild excitement after another—in poor, empty, idle hilarity and futile mirth—when manhood comes on with all its grave cares, they begin to occupy their minds with business. The mighty famine has begun. The man is beginning to find the emptiness of the pleasures for which he has lived. He can no longer enjoy them. The capacity for enjoyment is beginning to pass away from him; and now he plunges into business. He becomes a slave of daily routine, it may be. His mind is taken up with a thousand occupations. He begins to work hard, and all to satisfy

THE MORAL HUNGER OF HIS NATURE.

He gives himself up to money making, yet that does not satisfy, but he thinks it will. He flies to speculation: that excites, but does not satisfy—he hopes it will. He betakes himself to domestic occupations, the joys or the cares of family life, and he hopes to find satisfaction there; yet he does not. Is not that man a sensible being?

The mighty famine becomes more and more insupportable, and the want becomes more and more appalling. Our young friend sits solitary in the field. Can't you see him? His clothes are torn into rags, his eyes are sunken in their sockets, his cheeks are hollow, his lips are parched and cracked; he looks like the very effigy of famine itself. The swine are feeding around him. He is gnawing at the very husks which the swine eat. "And no man gave unto him." What, no man? no man. Of all his former friends, of those who had stood by him so faithfully as long as he had money to spend and luxuries to offer, what! no man? Not that boon companion, not that friend that only a few weeks ago swore that he would stand by him through thick and thin? No man? None.

The last crust has been devoured. There he sits famine-stricken, solitary, the prey of hunger in his body, far more the prey of remorse in his soul! There he sits. Poor "sensible" man! that is what his common sense has brought him to.

At this moment a change takes place. Holy Scripture describes it as a change from insanity to sanity. He ceases to be a lunatic, and he begins to be himself. "He came to himself." There passes from him, like a horrible dream, that strange delirium of the life which he had been leading since he left his father's home, with all its transient circumstances, its fleeting joys, its gaudy decorations, the poor, empty bubbles that have broken in his grasp—it has all passed from him like a horrible dream. He starts, as from a horrible nightmare. Can't you see him as he springs from the ground, with a sudden light beaming upon his countenance, his face turned toward the home of his infancy?

"What a fool I have been! My whole life has been one great mistake. From beginning to end, I have just been adding error to error as well as sin to sin. I have thrown away health, and affluence, and comfort, and respectability, and peace of mind, and innocency, and reputation, everything worth having—I have lost it all! And here I am, a wreck of a man, all real pleasure gone out of my life, stricken down with the fatal pestilence of sin, shriveled up by a miserable famine which reigns within my nature. What a fool I am!"

O, happy they who come to this conclusion before it is too late! I cannot help fearing that some of our "sensible" men never wake up from their dream of insanity until the last awful moment of their earthly experiences arrive; and then, when death is drawing near, eternity opening upon them—then you know, dear friends, it is too late to "come to ourselves." The agony that distorts the countenance of the dying, the horror that pales the cheeks and blanches the lips, can never recall so much as one single opportunity. If you "come to yourself" on your death-bed, just when you are going into eternity, it will simply be an anticipation of the pangs of your hell; you will simply antedate the torments of remorse which are already waiting for you. Thank God! we may "come to ourselves" now. Hast thou not found out that after all the Psalmist is right when he says, "Man walketh in a vain shadow, and disquieteth himself in vain"? Have you started out of your death-dream and suddenly discovered that you are on the brink of eternity unprepared, that you have wasted your talents, and squandered your substance, and injured your own nature, sinned against your own interest, and wounded the heart of your God?

This young man first "came to himself" with regard to the past. He had thought previously that he was acting "sensibly"; now he sees that he has been

PLAYING THE FOOL.

He has been trying all along to persuade himself that he has really been enjoying himself; now he suddenly comes to the conclusion that all the while he has been a stranger to real happiness. He looks at those four, or five, or six years. Before, he had plumed himself upon the life he had been leading; now, he scarcely dares to think of it. He hides his face with shame; he buries it in his hands, as he sits there in the field, the hot tears streaming through his fingers—

"What a fool I have been! What a wretch I have been! What a base ingrate I have been! Good God! wert Thou to strike me down with a thunderbolt of displeasure to the very depths of hell, it is only what I deserve."

And he "comes to himself" with regard to the present. He finds himself

FACE TO FACE WITH DEATH.

Nearer and nearer the grim specter draws, the bow seems already bent, and the arrow seems already fixed, and in a moment the fatal shaft may fly, and his mortal career may end in doom. Face to face with death—it is an awful thing! He feels it in his own body. That strange numbness that is creeping over him, that sense of mortal weakness, that stupor which has already been paralyzing the senses—what is it? incipient death. His strength has passed into weakness. He can scarcely totter across the field. His haggard form seems more fit for a sepulcher than for human society. What can he do? Whatever he can do he must do quickly. The tide of life is ebbing fast; a few more hours, and his opportunity will be gone. It is a long way to the country he has left, a long way to his father's house; if anything is to be done, not so much as a moment must be lost.

And thus it is that he also "comes to himself" with regard to the future. The future! what can he do? What hope is there for him? Has he not lost every chance, and thrown away every possibility? Nay, it strikes him that there is just

A FAINT RAY OF HOPE:

it seems a very faint one. Is there a possibility that he may get some relief from his friends in this distant land? No, he has given that up altogether. Can he not find a better master somewhere? No, he has tried all through the famine-stricken country, and this man who has sent him into the fields to feed swine is the best that he can find. What can he do? Can he work any harder? No, he has no strength left to work.

Where is hope to be found? Where is that ray of dim, uncertain light coming from? There rises up within his recollection the memory of a peaceful home, of calm, happy days. The bright sunlight of his childhood returns on his memory like a pleasant dream amidst the frightful horrors of his present experience. Could he regain it! could he retrace his steps, and get one more look at that dear old place! could he but sit down amongst the "hired servants" of his father's house!

My friends, he not only "comes to himself" with regard to himself, but also with regard to his father. He has taken a wrong view of his father—a distorted view. He had painted him in the most repulsive colors. Now he takes a different view of the case, and comes to the conclusion that after all he was wrong. He had wronged those hoary hairs. The thought rises in his mind:

"He loved me. Yes, he loved me after all. I saw the tear start into his eye when I left home. He wrung my hand when I went away from him, and his lip was quivering. Though I have given him so much trouble, I know he loved me. He was never hard on me. When, as a child, I wanted anything reasonable, it was always within my reach. If I had childish troubles, those kind, fatherly hands were laid upon my brow, and fatherly words of tenderness were spoken in my ear. Yes, he did love me. I have wronged him. I had no right to think him hard. He was not hard. I wonder if he is changed? Years have passed over him, years have passed over me. I left him with a smiling countenance. I put on my best appearance, and tried to seem as though I did not care a straw for leaving him. Perhaps he has hardened his heart against me, and will never look at me again. Yet perhaps there is something like love in his heart towards me still. Surely he cannot have altogether ceased to love his poor, wandering boy."

So he starts to his feet, and in another moment the word of resolution has sped forth from his lips,

"I will arise and go to my father."

It is even so with thee, awakened sinner. So soon as God begins to awaken thee, He awakens thee first of all *with regard to the past*.

Are you not awakened in regard to the past? You used to look upon it with complacency; now you look upon it with horror. You used to think well of yourself; now you cannot speak of yourself too hardly. There was a time when you flattered yourself that, at any rate, you were no worse than any other people; now it seems as if you could not invent any epithet sufficiently strong to indicate your horror and disgust at your past life. How is it?

You are beginning to "come to yourself," too, *with regard to your present*. You find yourself face to face with death. Spiritual death has already grasped you. Its iron clutch is on you. That dread specter is looking you in the face. You are beginning to realize, in your own terrible experience, the force of the words, "Dying, thou shalt die!" Do what you will, you cannot writhe out of the grasp of that terrible spiritual arrest. "O wretched man that I am! who shall deliver me from the body of this death?"

And you come to yourself *with respect to the future.* "Is there a possibility that I can be otherwise? May I turn my back upon the past? Is it possible that a sinner like myself can lead a new life? May even I become a new creature?"

Then it is that the soul begins to "come to itself" *with respect to the character of our heavenly Father.* Ah! my dear friends, you may have maligned Him, you may have slandered Him, you may have allowed Satan to misrepresent Him to your own fancy. You may have conceived of Him "as an austere man, reaping where he had not sown, and gathering where he had not strewed." It seems as though you could not speak too harshly of Him. But all that has changed, and you are beginning to come to the conclusion that

AFTER ALL HE IS YOUR FATHER,

that He has a Father's tenderness, pity and love; that although you have misrepresented Him so long, and sinned against Him so grossly, yet there must be something in that heart of His that goes out towards your misery. Ah! my friend, you are only just beginning to "come to yourself" about that Father: but if you will go a little nearer to that Father's house, bare your bosom to that Father's influence, if you will expose yourself to that Father's eye, it will not be long before you will have a different estimate from what you have even this moment of what that Father's love really is. Think not of God the Father as if He were unsympathetic. Believe what Christ Himself has taught of His Father's love: "God so loved the world that He gave His Son."

It was with a trembling step that the prodigal returned towards home; but, thank God, we may lay our fears aside. We need not tremble. We may feel perfectly sure what the nature of the Father's character is.

"He saw him afar off." Long before the prodigal saw the father, the father saw the prodigal. He must have been watching for him somewhere; standing at the window of his house, perhaps, gazing towards the distant land, thinking: "Will he come back, that wandering boy of mine? Will he return to his father's house? Is there chance of my seeing him again?"

Yes, all the time long he has been waiting and longing, longing and waiting. At last he sees a figure in the distance. It does not look like the same bright, happy boy that left his home a few years before, but it is the same. The father's heart goes out towards him. In another moment the father's feet are speeding to meet him. The *father* has no need to come to himself. He has been himself all the time. His heart has never changed, his love has never ceased, his pity has never failed. He flies on the very wings of love to meet the poor returning wretch. His rags do not repel him. His filth does not drive him back. Nay, nay, he casts his arms about his neck, clasps him in the embrace of affection. Hot tears stream down his cheeks.

"This, my son," he cries in triumph, as though he were a hero, instead of a reprobate, "This, my son, was dead, and is alive again; was lost, and is found."

Sinner, are you tired of that land of famine? Are you tired of wasting your substance,—tired of living as you have lived,—tired of sinning against your own interest,—tired of wandering from one poor folly to another,—from one empty occupation to another? Are you tired of seeking to satisfy the hunger of your soul with the miserable husks which are only fit for swine? If so then yield yourself up to the influences of that blessed Spirit who would bring you to yourself now.

O God, our God, may the prodigals come to themselves now! May they start up from their death swoon! May they see themselves as they really are! May they turn their backs upon the land of their shame, and may they turn their faces towards their Father's house! Father of spirits, fetch home Thy wandering ones now. Call them by Thy love. Woo them by Thy mercy. Bring them by Thy power. Let the joyful chorus be, "This Thy son was dead, and is alive again; was lost and is found!"

THE PRODIGAL'S RESOLVE | By T. DEWITT TALMAGE

There is nothing like hunger to take the energy out of a man. A hungry man can toil neither with pen nor hand nor foot. There has been many an army defeated not so much for lack of ammunition as for lack of bread. It was that fact that took the fire out of this young man of the parable. Storm and exposure will wear out any man's life in time, but hunger makes quick work. The most awful cry ever heard on earth is the cry for bread.

A traveler tells us that in Asia Minor there are trees which bear fruit looking very much like the long bean of our time. It is called the carob. Once in a while the people, reduced to destitution, would eat these carobs, but generally the carobs spoken of in this story were thrown only to the swine, and they crunched them with great avidity. But this young man could not even get these without stealing them. So one day, amid the swine troughs, he begins to soliloquize. He says:

"These are no clothes for a rich man's son to wear. This is no kind of business for me to be engaged in, feeding swine. I'll go home; I'll go home. I will arise and go to my father."

I know there are a great many people who try to throw a fascination, a romance, a halo about sin; but notwithstanding all that Lord Byron and George Sand have said in regard to it, it is a mean, low, contemptible business; and putting food and fodder into the troughs of a herd of iniquities that root and wallow in the soul of man is a very poor business for men and women intended to be sons and daughters of the Lord Almighty; and when this young man resolved to go home, it was a very wise thing for him to do, and the only question is whether we will follow him.

Satan promises large wages if we will serve him; but he clothes his victims with rags, and he pinches them with hunger, and when they start out to do better he sets after them all the bloodhounds of hell. Satan comes to us today and he promises all luxuries and emoluments if we will only serve him. Liar, down with thee to the pit! "The wages of sin is death." Oh! the young man of the text was wise when he uttered the resolution, "I will arise and go to my father."

In the time of Mary, the persecutor, a persecutor came to a Christian woman who had hidden in her house for the Lord's sake one of Christ's servants, and the persecutor said:

"Where is that heretic?"

The Christian woman said: "You open that trunk and you will see the heretic."

The persecutor opened the trunk, and on top of the linen in the trunk he saw a mirror. He said: "There is no heretic here."

"Ah!" she said, "you look in the mirror and you will see the heretic."

As I take up the mirror of God's Word, I would that, instead of seeing the prodigal of the text, we might see ourselves—our want, our wandering, our sin, our lost condition, so that we might be as wise as this young man was, and say: "I will arise and go to my Father."

The resolution of this text was formed in

DISGUST AT HIS PRESENT CIRCUMSTANCES.

If this young man had been, by his employer, set to culturing flowers, or training vines over an arbor, or keeping account of the pork market, or overseeing other laborers, he would not have thought of going home; if he had had his pockets full of money, if he had been able to say,

"I have a thousand dollars now of my own; what's the use of my going back to my father's house? Do you think I'm going back to apologize to the old man? Why, he would put me on the limits. He would not have going on around the old place such conduct as I have been engaged in. I won't go home. I have plenty of money, plenty of pleasant surroundings. Why should I go home?"

Ah! it was his pauperism, it was his beggary. He *had* to go home.

Some man comes and says to me: "Why do you talk about the ruined state of the human soul? Why don't you speak about the progress of the nineteenth century, and talk of something more exhilarating?"

It is for this reason: A man never wants the gospel until he realizes he is in a famine-struck state.

Suppose I should come to your home, and you are in good, sound, robust health, and I should begin to talk about medicines, and about how much better this medicine is than that, and some other medicine than some other medicine, and talk about this physician and that physician. After awhile you would get tired, and you would say:

"I don't want to hear about medicines. Why do you talk to me about physicians? I never have a doctor."

But suppose I come into your house and find you severely sick, and I know the medicines that will cure you, and I know the physician who is skillful enough to meet your case. You say:

"Bring on all that medicine, bring on that physician. I am terribly sick, and I want help."

If I come to you and you feel you are all right in body, and all right in mind, and all right in soul, you have need of nothing; but suppose I have persuaded you that the leprosy of sin is upon you,

THE WORST OF ALL SICKNESS.

Oh! then you say: "Bring me that balm of the gospel, bring me that divine medicament, bring me Jesus Christ."

"But," says someone, "how do you know that we are in a condition ruined by sin?"

Well, I can prove it in two ways, and you may have your choice. I can prove it either by the statement of men, or by the statement of God. Which shall it be?

You say, "Let us have the statement of God."

Well, He says in one place, "The heart is deceitful above all things and desperately wicked." He says in another place, "What is man that he should be clean? and he which is born of a woman, that he should be righteous?" He says in another place, "There is none that doeth good—no, not one." He says in another place, "As by one man sin entered into the world, and death by sin, and so death passed upon all men, for that all have sinned."

"Well," you say, "I am willing to acknowledge that; but why should I take the particular rescue that you propose?"

This is the reason: "Except a man be born again, he cannot see the kingdom of God." This is the reason: there is one name given under heaven among men, whereby they may be saved.

Then there are a thousand voices ready to say: "Well, I am ready to accept this help of the gospel. I would like to have this divine cure. How shall I go to work?"

Let me say that a mere whim, an undefined longing amounts to nothing. You must have a stout, a tremendous resolution like this young man of the text when he said: "I will arise and go to my father."

"Oh," says some young man, "how do I know my father wants me? How do I know if go back, I would be received?"

"Oh," says some young man, "you don't know where I have been. You don't know how far I have wandered. You wouldn't talk that way to me if you knew all the iniquities I have committed."

What is that flutter among the angels of God? What is that horseman running with quick dispatch? It is news, it is news! Christ has found the lost!

> *Nor angels can their joy contain,*
> *But kindle with new fire.*
> *"The sinner lost is found," they sing,*
> *And strike the sounding lyre.*

When Napoleon talked of going into Italy, they said:

"You can't get there. If you knew what the Alps were, you wouldn't talk about it or think about it. You can't get your ammunition-wagons over the Alps."

Then Napoleon rose in his stirrups, and, waving his hand toward the mountains, he said,

"There shall be no Alps!"

That wonderful pass was laid out, which has been the wonderment of all the years since—the wonderment of all engineers. And you tell me there are such mountains of sin between your soul and God, there is no mercy? Then I see Christ waving His hand toward the mountains. I hear Him say:

"I will come over the mountains of thy sin and the hills of thine iniquity."

There shall be no Pyrenees; there shall be no Alps.

Again: I notice that this resolution of the young man of my text was founded in sorrow at his misbehavior.—It was not mere physical plight. It was grief that he had so

MALTREATED HIS FATHER.

It is a sad thing after a father has done everything for a child to have that child ungrateful.

> *How sharper than a serpent's tooth it is,*
> *To have a thankless child.*

That is Shakespeare.

"A foolish son is the heaviness of his mother." That is the Bible.

Well, my friends, have not some of us been cruel prodigals? Have you not maltreated our Father? And such a Father! Three times a day He fed thee. He has poured sunlight into thy day and at night kindled up all the street lamps of heaven. With what varieties of apparel He hath clothed thee for the season! Whose eye watches thee? Whose hand defends thee? Whose heart sympathizes with thee? Who gave you your children? Who is guarding your loved ones departed? Such a Father! So loving, so kind.

If He had been a stranger; if He had forsaken us; if He had flagellated us; if He had pounded us and turned us out of doors on the commons, it would not have been so wonderful—our treatment of Him; but He is a Father, so loving, so kind, and yet how many of us for our wanderings have never apologized! If we say anything that hurts our friend's feelings, if we do anything that hurts the feelings of those in whom we are interested, how quickly we apologize! We can scarcely wait until we get pen and paper to write a letter of apology. How easy it is for anyone who is intelligent, right-hearted, to write an apology, or make an apology! We apologize for wrongs done to our fellows; but some of us perhaps have committed ten thousand times ten thousand wrongs against God, and never apologized. I remark still further, that this resolution of the text was founded in a feeling of

HOMESICKNESS.

I do not know how long this young man, how many months, how many years, he had been away from his father's house, but there is something about the reading of my text that makes me think he was homesick. Some of my readers know what that feeling is. Far away from home sometimes, surrounded by everything bright and pleasant—plenty of friends—you have said:

"I would give the world to be home tonight."

Well, this young man was homesick for his father's house. I have no doubt when he thought of his father's house he said:

"Now, perhaps father may not be living."

We read nothing in this story—this parable—founded on everyday-life—we read nothing about the mother. It says nothing about going home to her. I think she was dead. I think she had died of a broken heart at his wanderings, or, perhaps he had gone into dissipation from the fact that he could not remember a loving and sympathetic mother. A man never gets over having lost his mother. Nothing said about her, but he is homesick for his father's house. He thought he would just like to go and see if things were as they used to be. Many a man after having been off a long while has gone home and knocked at the door, and a stranger has come. It is the old homestead, but a stranger comes to the door. He finds out father is gone, and mother is gone; and brothers and sisters all gone. I think this young man of the text said to himself:

"Perhaps father may be dead."

Still he starts to find out. He is homesick. Are there any readers of mine homesick for God, homesick for heaven?

A sailor, after having been long on the sea, returned to his father's house, and his mother tried to persuade him not to go away again. She said:

"Now, you had better stay at home. Don't go away. We don't want you to go. You will have it a great deal better here."

But it made him angry. The night before he went away again to sea he heard his mother praying in the next room, and that made him more angry. He went far out on the sea, and a storm came up, and he was ordered to very perilous duty, and he ran up the ratlines, and amid the shrouds of the ship he heard the voice that he had heard in the next room. He tried to whistle, he tried to rally his courage; but he could not silence the voice he had heard in the next room, and there in the storm and darkness he said:

"O, Lord! what a wretch I have been! What a wretch I am! Help me just now, Lord God."

And I thought among my readers there may be some who have the memory of a father's petition or a mother's prayer pressing mightily upon their soul, and that this hour they may make the same resolution I find in my text, saying:

"I will arise and go to my father."

A lad at Liverpool went out to bathe in the sea, went out too far, got beyond his depth, and he floated off. A ship bound for Dublin came along, and took him on board. Sailors are generally very generous fellows, and one gave him a jacket, and another gave him shoes. A gentleman passing along the beach at Liverpool found the lad's clothes, and took them home, and the father was heartbroken, the mother was heartbroken, at the loss of their child. They had heard nothing from him day after day, and they ordered the usual mourning for the sad event. But the lad took ship from Dublin and arrived in Liverpool the very day the mourning arrived. He knocked at the door. The father was overjoyed, and the mother overjoyed, at the return of their lost son.

Oh, my friends, have you waded out too deep? Have you waded down into sin? Have you waded from the shore? Will you come back? When you come back, will you come in the rags of your sin, or will you come robed in the Savior's righteousness? I believe the latter. Go home to your God today. He is waiting for you. Go home!

But I remark, the next characteristic of this resolution was, it was

IMMEDIATELY PUT INTO EXECUTION.

The context says, "He arose and came to his father."

The trouble in the nine hundred and ninety-nine times out of a thousand is that our resolutions amount to nothing, because we make them for some distant time. If I resolve to become a Christian next year, that amounts to nothing at all. If I resolve to become a Christian tomorrow, that amounts to nothing at all. If I resolve this day to become a Christian, that amounts to nothing at all. If I resolve after I go home today to yield my heart to God, that amounts to nothing at all. The only kind of resolution that amounts to anything is the resolution that is immediately put into execution.

There is a man who had the typhoid fever, and he said: "Oh! if I could get over this terrible distress; if this fever should depart; if I could be restored to health, I would all the rest of my life serve God."

The fever departed. He got well enough to walk around the block. He got well enough to go over to business. He is well today—as well as he ever was. Where is the broken vow?

There is a man who said, long ago: "If I could live to the year 1897, by that time I will have my business matters all arranged, and I will have time to attend to religion, and I will be a good, thorough, Christian." The year 1897 has come. January, February, March,—a fourth of the year gone. Where is that broken vow?

"Oh," says some man, "I'll attend to that when I get my character fixed up, when I can get over my evil habits. I am now given to strong drink"; or, says the man, "I am given to uncleanness" or, says the man, "I am given to dishonesty. "When I get over my present habits, then I'll be a thorough Christian."

My brother, you will get worse and worse until Christ takes you in hand. "Not the righteous, sinners Jesus came to call."

Oh, but you say, "I agree with you in all that, but I must put it off a little longer."

Do you know there were many who came just as near as you are to the kingdom of God and never entered it?

I was at Easthampton, and I went into the cemetery to look around, and in that cemetery there are twelve graves side by side—the graves of sailors. This crew, some years ago, in a ship, went into the breakers at Amagansett, about three miles away. My brother, then preaching at Easthampton, had been at the burial. These men of the crew came very near being saved. The people from Amagansett saw the vessel, and they shot rockets, and they sent ropes from the shore, and these poor fellows got into the boat, and they pulled mightily for the shore, but just before they got to the shore the rope snapped, and the boat capsized, and they were lost, their bodies afterwards being washed upon the beach. Oh! what a solemn day it was—I have been told of it by my brother—when these twelve men lay at the foot of the pulpit, and he read over them the funeral service. They came very near the shore—within shouting distance of the shore, yet did not arrive on solid land.

There are some men who come almost to the shore of God's mercy, but not quite. To be *almost saved* is to be *lost*!

I will tell you of two prodigals—the one who got back and the other who did not get back.

In Richmond, Va., there is a very prosperous and beautiful home in many respects. A young man wandered off from that home. He wandered very far into sin. They heard of him after, but he was always on the wrong track. He would not go home. At the door of that beautiful home one night there was a great outcry. The young man of the house ran down to open the door, to see what was the matter. It was midnight. The rest of the family were asleep. There were the wife and children of this prodigal young man. The fact was he had come home and driven them out. He said:

"Out of this house! Away With these children! I will dash their brains out. Out into the storm!"

The mother gathered them up and fled.

The next morning the brother, the young man who had stayed at home, went out to find this prodigal brother and son, and he came where he was, and saw the young man wandering up and down in front of the place where he had been staying. The young man who had kept his integrity said to the older brother:

"Here, what does all this mean? What is the matter with you? Why do you act in this way?"

The prodigal looked at him and said: "Who am I? Who do you take me to be?"

He said, "You are my brother."

"No, I am not. I am a brute. Have you seen anything of my wife and children? Are they dead? I drove them out last night in the storm. I am a brute. John, do you think there is any help for me? Do you think I will ever get over this life of dissipation?" He added: "John, there is one thing that will stop this."

The prodigal ran his fingers across his throat, and said: "That will stop it, and I will stop it before night. Oh, my brain! I can stand it no longer."

That prodigal never got home. But I will tell you of another prodigal that did get home.

In England two young men started from their father's house and went down to Portsmouth—I have been there—a beautiful seaport. The father could not pursue his children—for some reason he could not leave home—and so he wrote a letter to Mr. Griffin, saying:

"Mr. Griffin, I wish you would go and see my two sons. They have arrived in Portsmouth, and they are going to take ship and are going away from home. I wish you would persuade them to come back."

Mr. Griffin went and tried to persuade them to return. He succeeded with one. He went with very easy persuasion, because he was very homesick already.

The other young man said: "I will not go. I have had enough of home. I'll never go home."

"Well," said Mr. Griffin, "then if you won't go home, I'll get you a respectable position on a respectable ship."

"No, you won't," said the prodigal. "No, you won't, I'm going as a common sailor; that will plague my father most, and what will do most to tantalize and worry him will please me best."

Years passed on, and Mr. Griffin was seated 1n his study one day when a messenger came to him, saying there was a young man in irons on a ship at the dock, condemned to death, and he wished to see this clergyman. Mr. Griffin went down to the dock and went on shipboard.

The young man said to him: "You don't know me, do you?"

"No," said he, "I don't know you."

"Don't you remember that young man you tried to persuade to go home, and he wouldn't go?"

"Oh, yes," said Mr. Griffin, "are you that man?"

"Yes, I am that man," said the other. "I would like to have you pray for me. I have committed murder, and I must die; but I don't want to go out of this world until some one prays for me. You are my father's friend, and I would like to have you pray for me."

Mr. Griffin went from judicial authority to judicial authority to get that young man's pardon. He slept not night or day. He went from influential person to influential person, until in some way he got that young man's pardon. He came down on the dock, and as he arrived with the pardon, the father came. He had heard that his son, under a disguised name, had committed a crime, and was going to be put to death. So Mr. Griffin and the father went on the ship's deck, and at the very moment Mr. Griffin offered the pardon to the young man the old father threw his arms around his son's neck,

The son said: "Father, I have done very wrong, and I am very sorry. I wish I had never broken your heart. I am very sorry."

"Oh," said the father, "don't mention it! It won't make any difference now. It is all over. I forgive you, my son," and he kissed him and kissed him and kissed him.

Now, I offer you the pardon of the gospel—full pardon, free pardon. I do not care what your crime has been. Though you say you have committed a crime against God, against your own soul, against your fellowmen, against your family, against the day of judgment, against the cross of Christ—whatever your crime has been, here is pardon, full pardon; and the very moment you take that pardon, your Heavenly Father throws His arms round about you and says:

"My son, I forgive you. It is all right. You are as much in my favor now as if you had never sinned."

Oh, there is joy on earth and joy in heaven! Who will take the Father's embrace?

THE TURNING POINT | By C. H. SPURGEON

"And he arose, and came to his father."

This sentence expresses the true turning point in the prodigal's life story. Many other matters led up to it, and before he came to it there was much in him that was very hopeful; but this was the point itself, and had he never reached it he would have remained a prodigal, but would never have been the prodigal restored, and his life would have been a warning rather than instruction to us. "He arose, and came to his father."

1. HERE WAS ACTION.

"He arose, and came to his father." He had already been in a state of thoughtfulness; he had come to himself, but now he was to go further, and come to his father. He had considered the past, and weighed it up, and seen the hollowness of all the world's pleasures; he had seen his condition in reference to his father, and his prospects if he remained in the far-off country; he had thought upon what he ought to do, and what would be the probable result of such a course; but now he passed beyond the dreaminess of thought into matter-of-fact acting and doing.

How long will it be, dear reader, before you will do the same? We are glad to have you thoughtful; we hope that a great point is gained when you are led to consider your ways, to ponder your condition, and to look earnestly into the future, for thoughtlessness is the ruin of many a traveler to eternity, and by its means the unwary fall into the deep pit of carnal security and perish therein.

But some of you have been among the "thoughtful" quite long enough; it is time you passed into a more practical stage. It is high time that you came to action. It would have been better if you had acted already; for, in the matter of reconciliation to God, first thoughts are best. When a man's life hangs on a thread, and hell is just before him, his path is clear, and a second thought is superfluous. The first impulse to escape from danger and lay hold on Christ is that which you would be wise to follow. Some of you whom I now address have been thinking, and thinking, and thinking, till I fear you will think yourselves into perdition. May you, by divine grace, be turned from thinking to believing, or else your thoughts will become the undying worm of your torment.

The prodigal had also passed beyond mere *regret*. He was deeply grieved that he had left his father's house. He lamented his lavish expenditure upon wantonness and reveling. He mourned that the son of such a father should be degraded into a swineherd in a foreign land. But he now proceeded from regret to repentance, and bestirred himself to escape from the condition over which he mourned.

What is the use of regret if we continue in sin? By all means pull up the sluices of your grief if the floods will turn the wheel of action, but you may as well reserve your tears, if they mean no more than idle sentimentalism. What avails it for a man to say he repents of his misconduct if he still perseveres in it? We are glad when sinners regret their sin and mourn the condition into which sin has brought them, but if they go no further, their regrets will only prepare them for eternal remorse.

Had the prodigal become inactive through despondency, or stolid through sullen grief, he must have perished, far away from his father's home, as it is to be feared many will whose sorrow for sin leads them into a proud unbelief and willful despair of God's love;

but he was wise, for he shook off the drowsiness of his despondency, and, with resolute determination, "arose and came to his father." Oh, when will you sad ones be wise enough to do the same? When will your thinking and your sorrowing give place to practical obedience to the gospel?

The prodigal also pressed beyond mere *resolving*. That is a sweet verse which says, "I will arise," but that is far better which says, "And he arose." Resolves are good, like blossoms; but actions are better, for they are the fruits. We are glad to hear from you the resolution, "I will turn to God," but holy angels in heaven do not rejoice over resolutions, they reserve their music for sinners who actually repent.

Many like the son in the parable have said, "I go, sir," but they have not gone. They are as ready at forgetting as they are at resolving. Every earnest sermon, every death in their family, every funeral knell for a neighbor, every pricking of conscience, every touch of sickness, sets them resolving to amend, but their promissory notes are never honored, their repentance ends in words. Their goodness is as the dew, which at early dawn hangs each blade of grass with gems, but leaves the fields all parched and dry when the sun's burning heat is poured upon the pasture. They mock their friends and trifle with their own souls.

Have you not dallied long enough? Have you not lied unto God sufficiently? Should you not now give over resolving and proceed to the solemn business of your souls like men of common sense? You are in a sinking vessel, and the life-boat is near, but your mere resolve to enter it will not prevent your going down with the sinking craft. As sure as you are a living man, you will drown unless you take the actual leap for life.

"He arose and came to his father." Now, observe that this *action of the prodigal was immediate*, and without further parley. He did not go back to the citizen of that country and say:

"Will you raise my wages? If not, I must leave."

Had he parleyed he had been lost; but he gave his old master no notice; he cancelled his indentures by running away.

I would that every sinner who reads this would break their league with death and violate their covenant with hell, by escaping for their lives to Jesus, who receives all such runaways. We want neither leave nor license for quitting the service of sin and Satan, neither is it a subject which demands a month's consideration: in this matter instantaneous action is the surest wisdom Lot did not stop to consult the king of Sodom as to whether he might quit his dominions, neither did he consult the parish officers as to the propriety of speedily deserting his home; but with the angel's hand pressing them, he and his fled from the city. Nay, one fled not; she looked and lingered, and that lingering cost her her life! That pillar of salt is the eloquent monitor to us to avoid delays when we are bidden to flee for our lives. Sinner, dost thou wish to be a pillar of salt? Wilt thou halt between two opinions, until God's anger shall doom thee to final impenitence? Wilt thou trifle with mercy till justice smite thee? Up, man, and while thy day of grace continues, fly thou into the arms of love!

The text implies that *the prodigal aroused himself*, and put forth all his energies. It is said, "he arose." He had till then been asleep upon the bed of sloth, or the couch of presumption.

Men are not saved between sleeping and waking. "The kingdom of heaven suffereth violence, and the violent take it by force." Grace does not stupefy us, it but arouses us.

Surely, it is worth while making an awful effort to escape from eternal wrath. It is worth while summoning up every faculty and power and emotion and passion of your being, and saying to yourself,

"I cannot be lost; I will not be lost; I am resolved that I will find mercy through Jesus Christ."

The worst of it is, O sinners, ye are so sluggish, so indifferent, so ready to let things happen as they may. Sin has bewitched and benumbed you. You sleep as on beds of down and forget that you are in danger of hell fire. You cry, "A little more rest, and a little more slumber, and a little more folding of the arms to sleep," and so you sleep on, though your damnation slumbereth not. Would to God you could be awakened! It is not in the power of my words to arouse you; but may the Lord Himself alarm you, for never were men more in danger. Let but your breath fail, or your blood pause, and you are lost forever. Frailer than a cobweb is that life on which your eternal destiny depends. If you were wise, you would not give sleep to your eyes nor slumber to your eyelids till you had found your God and been forgiven. Oh, when will you come to a reaction? How long will it be ere you believe in Jesus? How long will you sport between the jaws of hell? How long dare you provoke the living God?

II. Secondly,

HERE WAS A SOUL COMING INTO ACTUAL CONTACT WITH GOD,—

"He arose and came to his father." It would have been of no avail for him to have arisen if he had not come to his father. This is what the sinner has to do, and what the Spirit enables him to do: namely, to come straight away to his God. It will be a grand day for you, O sinner, when you do the same. Go personally, directly, and at once to God in Christ Jesus.

Alas! there are many anxious souls who look to themselves. They sit down and cry,

"I want to repent; I want to feel my need; I want to be humble."

O man, get up! What are you at? Leave yourself and go to your father.

"Oh, but I have so little hope; my faith is very weak, and I am full of fears."

What matter your hopes or your fears while you are away from your Father? Your salvation does not lie within yourself, but in the Lord's good will to you. You will never be at peace till, leaving all your doubts and your hopes, you come to your God and rest in His bosom.

"Oh, but I want to conquer my propensities to sin, I want to master my strong temptations."

I know what it is you want. You want the best robe without your Father's giving it to you, and shoes on your feet of your own procuring. You do not like going in a beggar's suit and receiving all from the Lord's loving hand. But this pride of yours must be given up, and you must get away to God, or perish forever. You must forget yourself, or only remember yourself so as to feel that you are bad throughout, and no more worthy to be called God's son. Give yourself up as a sinking vessel that is not worth pumping, but must be left to go down, and get you into the life-boat of free grace. Think of God your Father, and of His dear Son, the one Mediator and Redeemer of the sons of men. There is your hope—to fly away from self and to reach your Father.

Sinner, your business is with God. Hasten to Him at once. You have nothing to do with yourself, or your own doings, or what others can do for you. The turning point of salvation is, "he arose and came to his father." There must be a real, living, earnest, contact: of your poor guilty soul with God, a recognition that there is a God, and that God can be spoken to, and an actual speech of your soul to Him through Jesus Christ, for it is only God in Christ Jesus that is accessible at all. Going thus to God we tell Him that we are all wrong, and want to be set right; we tell Him we wish to be reconciled to Him, and are ashamed that we should have sinned against Him; we then put our trust in His Son, and we are saved.

O soul, go to God: it matters not though the prayer you come with may be a very broken prayer, or even if it has mistakes in it, as the prodigal's prayer had when he said, "Make me as one of thy hired servants"; the language of the prayer will not signify so long as you really approach to God. "Him that cometh to me," says Jesus, "I will in no wise cast out"; and Jesus ever liveth to make intercession for them that come to God through Him.

III. Now, thirdly,

IN THAT ACTION THERE WAS AN ENTIRE YIELDING UP OF HIMSELF.

In the prodigal's case, his proud independence and self-will were gone. In other days he demanded his portion, and resolved to spend it as he pleased; but now he is willing to be as much under rule as a hired servant. He has had enough of being his own master, and is weary of the distance from God which self-will always creates. He longs to get into a child's true place, namely, that of dependence and loving submission. The great mischief of all was his distance from his father, and he now feels it to be so. His great thought is to remove that distance by humbly returning, for then he feels that all other ills will come to an end. He yields up his cherished freedom, his boasted independence, his liberty to think and do and say whatever he chose, and he longs to come under loving rule and wise guidance,

Sinner, are you ready for this? If so, come and welcome; your heavenly Father longs to press you to His bosom!

He gave up all idea of self-justification, for he said, "I have *sinned.*"

Before he would have said, "I have a right to do as I like with my own. Who is to dictate how I shall spend my own money? If I do sow a few wild oats, every young man does the same. I have been very generous, if nothing else; nobody can call me greedy. I am no hypocrite."

But now the prodigal boasts no longer. Not a syllable of self-praise falls from his lips; he mournfully confesses, "I have sinned against heaven and before thee."

Sinner, if you would be saved, you also must come down from your high places, and acknowledge your iniquity. Confess that you have done wrong, and do not try to extenuate your offence; do not offer apologies and make your case better than it is, but humbly plead guilty and leave your soul in Jesus' hands. Of two things, to sin or to deny the sin, probably to deny the sin is the worse of the two, and shows a blacker heart.

Acknowledge your fault, man, and tell your heavenly Father that if it were not for His mercy you would have been in hell, and that as it is you richly deserve to be there even now. Make your case rather blacker than it is, if you can; this I say because I know you cannot do any such thing. When a man is in the hospital it cannot be of any service to him to pretend to be better than he is; he will not receive any more medical attention on that account, but rather the other way, for the worse his case the more likely is the physician to give him special notice. Oh, sinner, lay bare before God thy sores, thy putrefying sores of sin, the horrid ulcers of thy deep depravity, and cry, "O Lord, have mercy upon me!" This is the way of wisdom. Have done with pride and self-righteousness, and make thy appeal to the undeserved pity of the Lord, and thou wilt speed.

The penitent also yielded up all his supposed rights and claims upon his father, saying, "I am not worthy to be called thy son."

He might have said, "I have sinned, but still I am thy child," and most of us would have thought it a very justifiable argument; but he does not say so, he is too humble for that. He owns, "I am no more worthy to be called thy son."

A sinner is really broken down when he acknowledges that if God would have no mercy on him, but cast him away forever, it would be no more than justice. That soul is not far from peace which has ceased arguing and submits to the sentence. Oh, sinner, I urge thee, if thou wouldst find speedy rest, go and throw thyself at the foot of the cross where God meets such as thou art, and say,

"Lord, here I am; do what thou wilt with me. Never a word of excuse will I offer, nor one single plea by way of extenuation, I am a mass of guilt and misery, but pity me, oh, pity me! No rights or claims have I. I have forfeited the rights of creatureship by becoming a rebel against Thee. I am lost and utterly undone before the bar of Thy justice. From that justice I flee and hide myself in the wounds of Thy Son. According to the multitude of Thy tender mercies, blot out my transgressions!"

IV. Notice further, and fourthly, that

IN THIS ACT THERE WAS A MEASURE OF FAITH IN HIS FATHER

—a measure, I say, meaning thereby not much faith, but some. A little faith saves the soul.

There was faith in his father's power. He said, "In my father's house there is bread enough and to spare."

Sinner, dost thou not believe that God is able to save thee; that through Jesus Christ He is able to supply thy soul's needs? Canst thou not get as far as this, "Lord, if thou wilt thou canst make me clean"?

The prodigal had also some faith in his father's readiness to pardon; for if he had not so hoped, he would never have returned to his father at all; if he had been sure that his father would never smile upon him, he would never have returned to him.

Sinner, do believe that God is merciful, for so He is. Believe, through Jesus Christ, that He willeth not the death of the sinner, but had rather that he should turn to Him and live; for as surely as God liveth, this is truth, and do not thou believe a lie concerning thy God. The Lord is not hard or harsh, but He rejoices to pardon great transgressions.

Ah, poor sinner, dost thou not believe that God will have mercy on thee if He can do so consistently with His justice? If thou believest that, I have good news to tell thee. Jesus Christ, His Son, has offered such an atonement that God can be just, and yet the justifier of him that believeth. He has mercy upon the vilest, and justifieth the ungodly, and accepteth the very chief of sinners through His dear Son. Oh, soul, have faith in the atonement! The atonement made by the personal sacrifice of the Son of God must be infinitely precious; believe thou that there is efficacy enough in it for thee. It is thy safety to fly to that atonement and cling to the cross of Christ, and thou wilt honor God by so doing. It is the only way in which thou canst honor Him. Thou canst honor Him by believing that He can save thee, even thee. The truest faith is that which believes in the mercy of God in the teeth of conscious unworthiness.

The penitent in the parable went to his father too unworthy to be called his son, and yet he said, "My father." Faith has a way of seeing the blackness of sin, and yet believing that God can make the soul as white as snow. It is not faith that says, "I am a little sinner, and therefore God can forgive me"; but that is faith which cries, "I am a great sinner, an accursed and condemned sinner, and yet, for all that, God's infinite mercy can forgive me, and the blood of Christ can make me clean."

Believe in the teeth of thy feelings, and in spite of thy conscience. Believe in God, though everything within thee seems to say, "He cannot save thee. He will not save thee." Believe in God, sinner, over the tops of mountain sins. Do as John Bunyan says he did, for he was so afraid of his sins and of the punishment thereof, that he could not but run into God's arms, and he said,

"Though He had held a drawn sword in His hands, I would have run on the very point of it rather than have kept away from Him." So do thou, poor sinner.

Believe thy God. Believe in nothing else, but trust thy God, and thou wilt get the blessing.

It is wonderful the power of faith over God. It binds His justice and constrains His grace. I do not know how to illustrate it better than by a little story. When a I walked down my garden some time ago I found a dog amusing himself among the flowers. I knew that he was not a good gardener, and no dog of mine, so I threw a stick at him and bade him begone. After I had done so, he conquered me, and made me ashamed of having spoken roughly to him, for he picked up my stick, and, wagging his tail right pleasantly, he brought the stick to me and dropped it at my feet. Do you think I could strike him or drive him away after that? No, I patted him and called him good names. The dog had conquered the man. And if you, poor sinner, dog as you are, can have confidence enough in God to come to Him just as you are, it is not in His heart to spurn you. There is an omnipotence in simple faith which will conquer even the divine Being Himself. Only do but trust Him as He reveals Himself in Jesus, and you shall find salvation.

V. In the next place,

THIS ACT OF COMING INTO CONTACT WITH GOD IS PERFORMED BY THE SINNER JUST AS HE IS.

I do not know how wretched the prodigal's appearance may have been, but I will be bound to say he had grown none the sweeter by having fed swine, nor do I suppose his garments had been very sumptuously embroidered by gathering husks for them from the trees. Yet, just as he was, he came. Surely he might have spent an hour profitably in cleansing his flesh and his clothes, But no, he said, "I will arise," and no sooner said than done! He did arise, and he came to his father.

Every moment that a sinner stops away from God in order to get better he is but adding to his sin, for the radical sin of all is his being away from God, and the longer he stays in it the more he sins. The attempt to perform good works apart from God is like the effort of a thief to set his stolen goods in order. His sole duty is to return them at once.

Moreover, there was nothing needed from the prodigal but to return to his father. When a child who has done wrong comes back, the more its face is blurred with tears the better. When a beggar asks for charity, the more his clothes are in rags the better. Are not rags and sores the very livery of beggars? I once gave a man a pair of shoes because he said he was in need of them; but after he had put them on and gone a little way I overtook him in a gateway taking them off in order to go barefooted again. I think they were patent leather, and what should a beggar do in such attire? He was changing them for old shoes, those that were suitable to his business.

A sinner is never so well arrayed for pleading as when he comes in rags. At his worst, the sinner, for making an appeal to mercy, is at his best. And so, sinners, there is no need for you to linger; come just as you are.

"But must we not wait for the Holy Spirit?"

Ah, beloved, he who is willing to arise and go to his Father has the Holy Spirit. It is the Holy Spirit who moves us to return to God, and it is the spirit of the flesh or of the devil that would bid us wait.

It is the turning point of a man's life when he calls on God for forgiveness and acceptance, wherever it is done, whether in a workshop, or in a saw-mill, or in a church, or in a tabernacle; it does not matter where. There is the point—the getting to God in Christ, giving all up, and by faith resting in the mercy of God.

VI. The last point of all is this:

THAT ACT WROUGHT THE GREATEST CONCEIVABLE CHANGE IN THE MAN.

He was a new man after that. Harlots, winebibbers, you have lost your old companion now! He has gone to his father, and his father's company and yours will never agree. A man's return to his God means his leaving the chambers of vice and the tables of riot. You may depend upon it, whenever you hear of a professing Christian living in uncleanness, he has not been living anywhere near his God. He may have talked a great deal about it, but God and unchastity never agree. If you have friendship with God, you will have no fellowship with the unfruitful works of darkness.

Now, too, the penitent has done with all degrading works to support himself. You will not find him feeding swine any more. He has got away from that bondage. No more pig-feeding for him!

There is a change in him in all ways. Now he has come to his father his pride is broken down. He no longer glories in that which he calls his own; all his glory is in his father's free pardoning love. He never boasts of what he has, for he owns nothing but what his father gives him; and though he is far better off than ever he was in his spendthrift days, yet he is as unassuming as a little child. He is a gentleman-commoner upon the bounty of his God, and lives from day to day by a royal grant from the table of the King of kings. Pride is gone, but content fills its room. He would have been contented to be one of the servants of the house, much more satisfied is he to be a child. He loves his father with a new love; he cannot even mention his name without saying:

"And he forgave me, he forgave me freely, he forgave me all, and he said, 'Bring forth the best robe and put it on him; put a ring on his hand and shoes on his feet.'"

Perhaps you are saying. "May I now go to God just as I am, and through Jesus Christ yield myself up; and will He forgive me?"

Dear brother, or dear sister, wherever you may be, *try it*. That is the best thing to do: *try it*; and if the angels do not set the bells in heaven ringing, God has altered from what

He has been, for I know He received poor sinners in the past, and He will receive them now.

The worst thing I dread about you is, lest you should say, "I will think of it." *Don't think of it. Do it!* Concerning this no more *thinking* is needed; but to *do* it. Get away to God. Is it not according to nature that the creature should be at peace with its Creator? Is it not according to your conscience? Is there not something within you which cries, "Go to God in Christ Jesus."

In the case of that poor prodigal, the famine said to him, "*Go home!*" Bread was dear, meat was scarce, he was hungry, and every pang of want said, "*Go home! Go home!*" When he went to his old friend the citizen, and he asked him for help, his scowling looks said, "Why don't you go home?"

There is a time with sinners when even their old companions seem to say, "We do not want you. You are too miserable and melancholy. Why don't you go home?" They sent him to feed swine, and the very hogs grunted, "*Go home!*" When he picked up those carob husks and tried to eat them, they crackled, "*Go home.*" He looked upon his rags, and they gaped at him, "*Go home.*" His hungry belly and his faintness cried, "*Go home.*" Then he thought of his father's face, and how kindly it had looked at him, and it seemed to say, "*Come home!*" He remembered the bread enough and to spare, and every morsel seemed to say, "*Come home!*" He pictured the servants sitting down to dinner and feasting to the full and every one of them seemed to look right away over the wilderness to him, and to say "*Come home!* Thy father feeds us well. Come home!" Everything said, "*Come home!*" Only the devil whispered, "Never go back. Fight it out! Better starve than yield! Die game!" But then he had got away from the devil this once, for he had come to himself, and he said:

"No; I will arise and go to my father."

Oh that you would be equally wise! Sinner, what is the use of being damned for the sake of a little pride? Yield man! Down with your pride! You will not find it so hard to submit if you remember that dear Father who loved us and gave Himself for us in the person of His own dear Son. You will find it sweet to yield to such a friend. And when you get your head in His bosom, and feel His warm kisses on your cheek, you will soon feel that it is sweet to weep for sin—sweet to confess your wrong doing, and sweeter still to hear Him say:

"I have blotted out thy sins like a cloud, and like a thick cloud thy transgressions." "Though your sins be as scarlet, they shall be as white as snow; though they be red like crimson, they shall be as wool."

God Almighty grant this may be the case with hundreds who read this. He shall have all the glory of it, but my heart shall be very glad, for I feel nothing but the greatest conceivable joy at the thought of making merry with you by and by, when you come to own my Lord and Master, and we sit together at the sacramental feast, rejoicing in His love. God bless you, for His sake. Amen.

THE RING FOR THE RETURNING PRODIGAL |
By T. DEWITT TALMAGE

I will not here rehearse the familiar story of the fast young man of the parable. You know what a splendid home he left. You know what a hard time he had. And you remember how, after that season of vagabondage and prodigality, he resolved to go and weep out his sorrows on the bosom of parental forgiveness.

Well, there is great excitement one day in front of the door of the old farm-house. The servants come rushing up, and say:

"What's the matter? What is the matter?"

But before they quite arrive, the old man cries out:

"Put a ring on his hand."

What a seeming absurdity! What can such a wretched mendicant as this fellow that is tramping on toward the house want with a ring? Oh, he is the prodigal son! No more tending of the swine-trough. No more longing for the pods of the carob tree. No more blistered feet. Off with the rags! On with the robe! Out with the ring! Even so does God receive every one of us when we come back.

There are gold rings, and pearl rings, and emerald rings, and diamond rings; but the richest ring that ever flashed on the vision is that which our Father puts upon a forgiven soul.

I know that the impression is broad among some people that religion bemeans and belittles a man; that it takes all the sparkle out of his soul; that he has to exchange a roistering independence for an ecclesiastical strait-jacket. No so. When a man becomes a Christian, he does not go down, he starts upward. Religion multiplies one by ten thousand. Nay, the multiplier is infinity. It is not a blotting out—it is a polishing, it is an arborescence, it is an efflorescence, it is an irradiation. When a man comes into the kingdom of God, he is not sent into a menial service, but the Lord God Almighty from the palaces of heaven calls upon the messenger angels that wait upon the throne to fly and "put a ring on his hand." In Christ are the largest liberty, and brightest joy, and highest honor, and richest adornment. "Put a ring on his hand."

I remark, in the first place, that when Christ receives a soul into His love. He puts upon him

THE RING OF HIS ADOPTION.

While in my church in Philadelphia, there came the representative of the Howard Mission of New York. He brought with him eight or ten children of the street that he had picked up, and he was trying to find for them Christian homes, and as the little ones stood on the pulpit and sang, our hearts melted within us.

At the close of the service a great-hearted wealthy—man came up and said,

"I'll take this little bright-eyed girl, and I'll adopt her as one of my own children"; and he took her by the hand, lifted her into his carriage, and went away.

The next day, while we were in the church gathering up garments for the poor of New York, this little child came back with a bundle under her arm, and she said,

"There's my old dress. Perhaps some of the poor children would like to have it."

She herself was in bright and beautiful array, and those who more immediately examined her said she had a ring on her hand. It was the ring of adoption.

There are a great many persons who pride themselves on their ancestry, and they glory over the royal blood that pours through their arteries. In their line there was a lord, or a duke, or a prime minister, or a king. But when the Lord, our Father, puts upon us the ring of His adoption, we become children of the Ruler of all nations. "Behold what manner of love the Father hath bestowed upon us, that we should be called the sons of God." It matters not how poor our garments may be in this world, or how scant our bread, or how mean the hut we live in; if we have the ring of Christ's adoption upon our hand we are assured of eternal defenses.

Adopted! Why, then, we are brothers and sisters to all the good of earth and heaven. We have the family name, the family dress, the family keys, the family wardrobe. The father looks after us, robes us, defends us, blesses us. We have royal blood in our veins, and there are crowns in our line. If we are His children, then princes and princesses. It is only a question of time when we get our coronet.

Adopted! Then we have the family secrets, "The secret of the Lord is with them that fear Him."

Adopted! Then we have the family inheritance, and in the day when our Father shall divide the riches of heaven, we shall take our share of the mansions and palaces and temples.

Henceforth let us boast no more of an earthly ancestry. The insignia of eternal glory is our coat of arms. This ring of adoption puts upon us all honor and all privilege. Now we can take the words of Charles Wesley, that prince of hymn-makers, and sing:

> *Come, let us join our friends above,*
> *Who have obtained the prize,*
> *And on the eagle wings of love*
> *To joy celestial rise.*

> *Let all the saints terrestrial sing*
> *With those to glory gone;*
> *For all the servants of our King,*
> *In heaven and earth are one.*

I have been told that when any of the members of any of the great secret societies of this country are in a distant city, and are in any kind of trouble, and are set upon by enemies, they have only to give a certain signal, and the members of that organization will flock around for defense. And when any man belongs to this great Christian brotherhood, if he gets into trouble, into trial, into persecution, into temptation, he has only to show this ring of Christ's adoption, and all the armed cohorts of heaven will come to his rescue.

Still further, when Christ takes a soul into His love He puts upon it

A MARRIAGE-RING.

Now, that is not a whim of mine. "I will betroth thee unto me forever; yea, I will betroth thee unto me in righteousness, and in judgment, and in loving kindness, and in mercies." (Hosea 2:19)

At the wedding altar the bridegroom, puts a ring upon the hand of the bride, signifying love and faithfulness. Trouble may come upon the household, and the carpets may go, the pictures may go, the piano may go, everything else may go—the last thing that goes is the marriage-ring, for it is considered sacred.

In the burial hour it is withdrawn from the hand and kept in a casket, and sometimes the box is opened on an anniversary day, and as you look at that ring you see under its arch a long procession of precious memories. Within the golden circle of that ring there is room for a thousand sweet recollections to revolve, and you think of the great contrast between the hour when, at the close of the "Wedding March," under the flashing lights and amid the aroma of orange blossoms, you set that ring on the round finger of the plump hand, and that hour when, at the close of the exclusive watching, when you knew that the soul had fled, you took from the hand, which gave back no responsive clasp, from that emaciated finger, the ring that she had worn so long and worn so well.

On some anniversary day you take up that ring, and you repolish it until all the old luster comes back, and you can see in it the flash of eyes that long ago ceased to weep.

Oh! it is not an unmeaning thing when I tell you that when Christ receives your soul into His keeping, He puts on it a marriage-ring. He endows you from that moment with all His wealth. You are one—Christ and the soul—one in sympathy, one in affection, one in hope. There is no power on earth or hell to effect a divorcement after Christ and the soul are united. Other kings have turned out their companions when they got weary of them, and sent them adrift from the palace gate. Ahasuerus banished Vashti; Napoleon forsook Josephine; but Christ is the husband that is true forever. Having loved you once, He loves you to the end. Did they not try to divorce Margaret, the Scotch girl, from Jesus? They said:

"You must give up your religion."

She said: "I can't give up my religion."

And so they took her down to the beach of the sea, and they drove in a stake at low water mark, and they fastened her to it, expecting that as the tide came up her faith would fail. The tide began to rise, and came up higher and higher, and to the girdle, and to the lip, and in the last moment, just as the waves were washing her soul into glory, she shouted the praises of Jesus.

Oh, no, you cannot separate a soul from Christ! It is an everlasting marriage. Battle and storm and darkness cannot do it. Is it too much exultation for a man, who is but dust and ashes like myself, to cry out this moment: "I am persuaded that neither height, nor depth, nor principalities, nor powers, nor things present, nor things to come, nor any other creature shall separate me from the love of God, which is in Christ Jesus my Lord"? Glory be to God that when Christ and the soul are married they are bound by a chain—a golden chain—if I might say so—a chain with one link, and that one link the golden ring of God's everlasting love!

I go a step further, and tell you that when Christ receives a soul into His love He puts on him

THE RING OF FESTIVITY.

You know that it has been the custom in all ages to bestow rings on very happy occasions. There is nothing more appropriate for a birthday gift than a ring. You delight to bestow such a gift upon your children at such a time. It means joy, hilarity, festivity.

Well, when this old man of the story wanted to tell how glad he was that his boy had got back, he expressed it in this way. Actually, before he ordered sandals to be put on his bare feet, before he ordered the fatted calf to be killed to appease the boy's hunger, he commanded:

"Put a ring on his hand."

Oh, it is a merry time when Christ and the soul are united! What a splendid thing it is to feel that all is right between my God and myself! What a glorious thing it is to have God just take up all the sins of my life, and put them in one bundle, and then fling them into the depths of the sea, never to rise again, never to be talked of again! Pollution all gone. Darkness all illumined. God reconciled. The prodigal home. "Put a ring on his hand."

Every day I find happy Christian people. I find some of them with no second coat, some of them in huts and tenement houses, not one earthly comfort afforded them; and yet they are as happy as happy can be. "They sing "Rock of Ages" as no other people in the world sing it. They never wore any jewelry in their life but one gold ring, and that was the ring of God's undying affection. Oh, how happy religion makes us! Did it make you gloomy and sad? Did you go with your head cast down? I do not think you got religion, my brother. That is not the effect of religion. True religion is a joy. "Her ways are ways of pleasantness, and all her paths are peace."

Religion lightens all our burdens. It smooths all our way. It interprets all our sorrows. It changes the jar of earthly discord for the peal of festal bells. In front of the flaming furnace of trial it sets the forge on which scepters are hammered out. Would you not like this hour to come up from the swine-feeding and try this religion? All the joys of heaven would come out and meet you, and God would cry from the throne: "Put a ring on his hand."

You are not happy. There is no peace, and sometimes you laugh when you feel a great deal more like crying. The world is a cheat. It first wears you down with its follies, then it kicks you out into darkness. It comes back from the massacre of a million souls to attempt the destruction of your soul today. No peace out of God, but here is the fountain that can slake the thirst. Here is the harbor where you can drop safe anchorage.

Would you not like, I ask you—not perfunctorily, but as one brother might talk to another—would you not like to have a pillow of rest to put your head on? And would you not like, when you retire at night, to feel that all is well, whether you wake up tomorrow morning at six o'clock, or sleep the sleep that knows no waking? Would you not like to exchange this awful uncertainty about the future for a glorious assurance of heaven? Accept of the Lord Jesus now, and all is well. If some peril should cross the street and dash your life out it would not hurt you. You would rise up immediately. You would stand in the celestial streets. You would be amid the great throng that forever worship and are forever happy. If this night some sudden disease should come upon you, it would not frighten you. If you knew you were going, you could give a calm farewell to your beautiful home on earth, and know that you are going right into the companionship of those who have already got beyond the toiling and the weeping.

You feel on Saturday night different from the way you feel any other night of the week. You come home from the bank, or the store, or the office, and you say:

"Well, now my week's work is done, and tomorrow is Sunday."

It is a pleasant thought. There is refreshment and reconstruction in the very idea. Oh, how pleasant it will be if, when we get through the day of our life, and we go and lie down in our bed of dust, we can realize:

"Well, now the work is all done, and tomorrow is Sunday—an everlasting Sunday."

> *Oh, when, thou city of my God,*
> *Shall I thy courts ascend,*
> *Where congregations ne'er break up,*
> *And Sabbaths have no end?*

Some who are very near the eternal world will read this. If you are Christians I bid you be of good cheer. Bear with you our congratulations to the bright city. Aged men, who will soon be gone, take with you our love for our kindred in the better land, and when you see them, tell them we are soon coming. Only a few more sermons to preach and hear. Only a few more heartaches. Only a few more toils. Only a few more tears. And then— what an entrancing spectacle will open before us!

> *Beautiful heaven, where all is light,*
> *Beautiful angels, clothed in white,*
> *Beautiful strains that never tire,*
> *Beautiful harps through all the choir,*
> *There shall I join the chorus sweet,*
> *Worshiping at the Savior's feet.*

And so I approach you now with a general invitation, not picking out here and there a man, or here and there a woman, or here and there a child; but giving you an unlimited invitation, saying:

"Come, for all things are now ready."

We invite you to the warm heart of Christ, and the enclosure of the Christian church. I know a great many think that the church does not amount to much—that it is obsolete, that it did its work and is gone now, so far as all usefulness is concerned. It is the happiest place I have ever been in except my own home.

I know there are some people who say they are Christians who seem to get along without any help from others, and who culture solitary piety. They do not want any ordinances. I do not belong to that class. I cannot get along without them. There are so many things in this world that take my attention from God, and Christ, and heaven, that I want all the helps of all the symbols and of all the Christian associations; and I want around about me a solid phalanx of men who love God and keep His commandments.

Reader, would you not like to enter into that association? Then by a simple, child-like faith, apply for admission into the visible church, and you will be received. No questions asked about your past history or present surroundings. Only one test—do you love Jesus?

Some have been thinking on this subject year after year. They have found out that this world is a poor portion. They want to be Christians. They have come almost into the kingdom of God; but there they stop, forgetful of the fact that to be almost saved is not to be saved at all. Oh, my brother, after having come so near to the door of mercy, if you turn back, you will never come at all! After all you have heard of the goodness of God, if you turn away and die, it will not be because you did not have a good offer.

God's spirit will not always strive
With hardened self-destroying man;
Ye who persist His love to grieve
May never hear His voice again.

May God Almighty this moment move upon your soul and bring you back from the husks of the wilderness to the Father's house, and set you at the banquet, and "put a ring on your hand."

BEAUTIFUL SNOW

O, the snow, the beautiful snow!
Filling the sky and the earth below;
Over the housetops, over the street,
Over the heads of the people you meet,
      Dancing,
           Flirting,
                Skipping along.
Beautiful snow! it can do no wrong,
Flying to kiss a fair lady's cheek,
Clinging to lips in a frolicsome freak—
Beautiful snow from the heavens above,
Pure as an angel, gentle as love!

O, the snow, the beautiful snow!
How the flakes gather, and laugh as they go
Whirling about in their maddening fun.
It plays in its glee with every one.
      Chasing,
           Laughing,
                Hurrying by,
It lights on the face, and it sparkles the eye;
And playful dogs with a bark and a bound
Snap at the crystals that eddy around.
The town is alive, and its heart is aglow
To welcome the coming of beautiful snow.

How wildly the crowd goes swaying along,
Hailing each other with humor and song!
How the gay sleds like meteors flash by,
Bright for the moment, then lost to the eye!
      Ringing,
           Swinging,
                Dashing they go
Over the crust of the beautiful snow—
Snow so pure, when it falls from the sky,
As to make one regret to see it lie
To be trampled and tracked by the thousand feet,
Till it blends with the filth in the horrible street.

Once I was pure as the snow, but I fell—
Fell like the snowflakes from heaven to hell;
Fell to be trampled as filth in the street;
Fell to be scoffed, to be spit on, and beat;
      Pleading,
          Cursing,
             Dreading to die;
Selling my soul to whoever would buy;
Dealing in shame for a morsel of bread;
Hating the living, and fearing the dead—
Merciful God! Have I fallen so low?
And yet I was once like the beautiful snow.

Once I was fair as the beautiful snow,
With an eye like its crystal, and heart like its glow
Once I was loved for my innocent grace,
Flattered and sought for the charms of the race.
      Father,
          Mother,
             Sisters, all,
God and myself I have lost by my fall!
The veriest wretch that goes shivering by
Will make a wide sweep lest I wander too nigh.
For all that is on or above me I know
There's nothing as pure as the beautiful snow.

How strange it should be that this beautiful snow
Should fall on a sinner with nowhere to go!
How strange it would be, when night comes again,
If the snow and the ice struck my desperate brain,
      Fainting,
          Freezing,
             Dying alone,
Too wicked for prayer, too weak for a moan
To be heard in the streets of the crazy town,
Gone mad in the joy of the snow coming down;
To be and to die in my terrible woe,
With a bed and a shroud of the beautiful snow.

Helpless and foul as the trampled snow,
Sinner despair not! Christ stoopeth low
To rescue the soul that is lost in its sin,

And raise it to life and enjoyment again.
    Groaning,
        Bleeding,
            Dying for thee,
The Crucified hung on the 'cursed tree.
His accents of mercy fall soft on thine ear.
Is there mercy for me? Will He heed my prayer?
O God, in the stream that for sinners did flow,
Wash me, and I shall be whiter than snow!
    — John Whitaker Watson

INFLUENCE OF HENRY MOOREHOUSE[1]

A NEW epoch in Mr. Moody's religious experience and preaching was marked by his friendship with Henry Moorehouse. The acquaintance made in Dublin during this first short visit to Great Britain seems to have been but casual.

"I had read in the papers about 'The Boy Preacher,'" said Mr. Moody in relating the circumstances of his meeting with Moorehouse, "but I did not know that this was he. He introduced himself to me and said he would like to come to Chicago to preach. He was a beardless boy—he didn't look more than seventeen—and I said to myself, 'He can't preach.' He wanted me to let him know what boat I was going to America on, as he would like to go on the boat with me.

"Well, I thought he couldn't preach and I didn't let him know. I hadn't been in Chicago a great many weeks before I got a letter saying that he had arrived in America and that he would come to Chicago and preach for me if I wanted him. Well, I sat down and wrote a very cold letter: 'If you come West, call on me.' I thought that would be the last I should hear of him. I soon got another letter saying he was still in the country, and would come to Chicago and preach for me if I wanted him. I wrote again, 'If you happen to come West, drop in on me.' In the course of a few days I got a letter stating that on a certain Thursday he would be in Chicago and would preach for me. Then what to do with him I didn't know. I had made up my mind that he couldn't preach. I was going to be out of town Thursday and Friday, and I told some of the officers of the church, 'There is an Englishman coming here Thursday who wants to preach. I don't know whether he can or not.'

"They said there was a great deal of interest in the church, and they did not think he had better preach then; he was a stranger, and he might do more harm than good. 'Well,' I said, 'you might try him. I will announce him to speak Thursday night. Your regular weekly meeting is on Friday. After hearing him you can either announce that he will speak again the next night or you can have your usual prayer-meeting. If he speaks well both nights you will know whether to announce him or me for the Sunday meetings. I will be back Saturday.'

"When I got back Saturday morning I was anxious to know how he got on. The first thing I said to my wife when I got in the house was, 'How is the young Englishman coming along? How do the people like him?'

"'They like him very much.'

"'Did you hear him?'

"'Yes.'

"'Well, did you like him?'

"'Yes, I liked him very much. He has preached two sermons from that verse of John, *"For God so loved the world, that He gave His only begotten Son, that whosoever believeth in Him should not perish, but have everlasting life,"* and I think you will like him, although he preaches a little differently from you.'

---

[1] From Chapter 14 of *The Life of Dwight L. Moody*, by His Son. Later editions removed this chapter, but it is a significant turning point in Mr. Moody's spiritual life, so is included here.

"'How is that?'

"'Well, he tells the worst sinners that God loves them.'

"'Then,' said I, 'he is wrong.'

"'I think you will agree with him when you hear him,' said she, 'because he backs up everything he says with the Bible.'

"Sunday came, and as I went to the church I noticed that everyone brought his Bible. The morning address was to Christians. I had never heard anything quite like it. He gave chapter and verse to prove every statement he made. When night came the church was packed. 'Now, beloved friends,' said the preacher, 'if you will turn to the third chapter of John and the sixteenth verse, you will find my text.' He preached the most extraordinary sermon from that verse. He did not divide the text into 'secondly' and 'thirdly' and 'fourthly'; he just took the whole verse, and then went through the Bible from Genesis to Revelation to prove that in all ages God loved the world. God had sent prophets and patriarchs and holy men to warn us, and then He sent His Son, and after they killed Him, He sent the Holy Ghost. I never knew up to that time that God loved us so much. This heart of mine began to thaw out; I could not keep back the tears. It was like news from a far country: I just drank it in. So did the crowded congregation. I tell you there is one thing that draws above everything else in this world, and that is *love*. A man that has no one to love him, no mother, no wife, no children, no brother, no sister, belongs to the class that commits suicide.

"It's pretty hard to get a crowd out in Chicago on a Monday night, but the people came. They brought their Bibles, and Moorehouse began, 'Beloved friends, if you will turn to the third chapter of John, and the sixteenth verse, you will find my text,' and again he showed on another line, from Genesis to Revelation, that God loved us. He could turn to almost any part of the Bible and prove it. Well, I thought that was better than the other one; he struck a higher note than ever, and it was sweet to my soul to hear it. He just beat that truth down into my heart, and I have never doubted it since. I used to preach that God was behind the sinner with a double-edged sword ready to hew him down. I have got done with that. I preach now that God is behind him with love, and he is running away from the God of love.

"Tuesday night came, and we thought he had surely exhausted that text and that he would take another, but he said: 'If you will turn to the third chapter of John and the sixteenth verse, you will find my text,' and he preached again from that wonderful text, and this night he seemed to strike a higher chord still. *'God so loved the world, that He gave His only begotten Son, that whosoever believeth in Him should not perish but have'*—not going to have when you die, but have it right here, now—*'eternal life.'* By that time we began to believe it, and we have never doubted it since.

"For six nights he had preached on this one text. The seventh night came, and he went into the pulpit. Every eye was upon him. He said, 'Beloved friends, I have been hunting all day for a new text, but I cannot find anything so good as the old one; so we will go back to the third chapter of John and the sixteenth verse,' and he preached the seventh sermon from those wonderful words, *'God so loved the world.'* I remember the end of that sermon: 'My friends,' he said, 'for a whole week I have been trying to tell you how much God loves you, but I cannot do it with this poor stammering tongue. If I could borrow Jacob's ladder and climb up into Heaven and ask Gabriel, who stands in the presence of the Almighty, to tell me how much love the Father has for the world, all he could say would be: *"God so loved the world, that He gave His only begotten Son, that whosoever believeth in Him should not perish, but have everlasting life."'*

"If a man gets up in that pulpit and gives out that text today, there is a smile all over the church."

Mr. Moorehouse taught Moody to draw his sword full length, to fling the scabbard away, and enter the battle with the naked blade.

This first visit to America was repeated in August, 1868, when he again visited Chicago and labored with Mr. Moody for two months, preaching in his church and in Farwell Hall. During this time, accompanied by Mr. Moody, he went to various other cities, holding some seventy-two meetings. In the winter of 1872 he came again to America and conducted services in Chicago, and again in 1878 he assisted Mr. Moody's evangelistic work in a New England mission.

Mr. Moorehouse was among the first to welcome Moody to England in June, 1875, and assisted him at Newcastle-on-Tyne, and other places, taking a leading part in his all-day meetings. The delighted recognition of each other's strength of character bound them closely together in a strong friendship. Mr. Moorehouse's affectionate nature and devotion to the Master and Mr. Moody's strong common sense and ever-widening influence combined to make them irresistible companions in evangelistic work.

www.ingramcontent.com/pod-product-compliance
Lightning Source LLC
Chambersburg PA
CBHW020606030426

42337CB00013B/1238